THE INSIDER'S GUIDE TO

B·A·L·I

THE INSIDER'S GUIDES

JAPAN • CHINA • KOREA • HONG KONG • BALI • THAILAND • INDIA • NEPAL • AUSTRALIA
HAWAII • CALIFORNIA • NEW ENGLAND • FLORIDA • MEXICO
THE SOVIET UNION • SPAIN • TURKEY • GREECE
KENYA

The Insider's Guide to Bali
First Published 1989
Hunter Publishing Inc
300 Raritan Center Parkway
CN94, Edison, N.J. 08818
by arrangement with CFW Publications Ltd

ISBN: 1-55650-053-X

Created, edited and produced by CFW Publications Ltd
130 Connaught Road C., Hong Kong. Fax (852) 543 8007
Editor in Chief: Allan Amsel
Picture editor and designer : Leonard Lueras
Original design concept: Hon Bing-wah
Text and artwork composed and information updated
using Xerox Ventura software

ACKNOWLEDGMENTS
The Author would like to acknowledge the kind assistance given him by many people, but
particularly by Russel Farr, Gede and Budi Sudantha, Mr Oka of Puri Anyar, Kerambitan, and
Doktorandus Rai of the Badung Tourist Office, Denpasar.

Photo Credits
Leonard Lueras: Title page; pp.9 top, 14-15, 16-19, 26, 34 left, 35 right, 36, 37, 52 bottom, 58, 59,
61, 66-67, 84-85, 89, 96-97, 100-101, 104-105, 114, 141, 149, 150, 162, 163, 181, 196-197, 201,
back cover bottom right
Rio Helmi: Front cover, pp. 20-21, 75, 88, 118, 142
Bradley Winterton, pp. 50-51, 52 top, 76, 184-5

Printed by Samhwa Printing Co Ltd, Seoul, Korea

THE INSIDER'S GUIDE TO

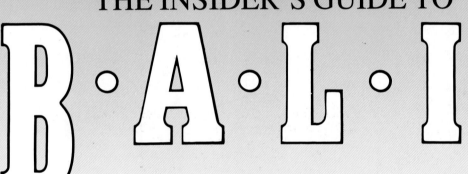

by Bradley Winterton

Photographed by Nik Wheeler

HUNTER PUBLISHING, INC.
Edison, N.J.

Contents

MAPS
Bali   6-7
North Bali   104-105
Sanur   110
Denpasar   113
South Bali and the Bukit   117
Kuta   125
Central Bali and the Heights   146-147
East Bali   167
Nusa Penida   180

THE ISLAND OF BALI   9
Volcanoes in the Ocean   11
    An Equable Climate • Tropic
    Landscape • From Java Man to
    Golkar • A Note on Language

THE CULTURE OF BALI   25
A Village Upbringing   27
    Banjar and Subak • The Cult of
    Rice • Where Do You Sit? • Naming
    of Names • Sex Roles • Birth,
    Childhood, Love and Marriage •
    Tooth-filing
Men and Gods   39
    Balinese Hinduism • Hotels for the
    Gods • Time Passes By • High Days •
    Three Festivals • A Village Cremation •
    Magic and Witchcraft • Heroes and
    Villains
The Balinese at Play   61
    Silver Rain • Dance and Drama •
    Shadows in the Dark • The Affrighted
    Sun • Cricket-fighting • Bird
    Orchestras
Arts and Crafts   82
    Painting • Wood-carving •
    The Other Face • Take-away Shrines •
    Endek, Ikat and Batik • Gold and
    Silver
Rijsttaffel to Kretek   90
    Festive Foods • Drinks • Tropical
    Fruits • Coconut Palms • Salt in the
    Wound • Betel • Jamu • Kretek

THE BROAD HIGHWAY   101
North Bali   103
    Bali's Old Capital: Singaraja • Black-
    sand Beaches: Lovina • Springs and
    Temples • Unheard Melodies • Gongs •
    Yeh Sanih • Village with a View
Sanur   110
    A Discreet Campari • Where to Stay •
    Where to Eat • Nightlife • Shopping •
    An Explosion of Paint
Bali's Capital: Denpasar   112
    Heroic Last Stand • Art and
    Information • Where to Stay • Where
    to Eat • Shopping • Transport
Nusa Dua and the Bukit   116
    In Praise of Limestone • Five-star
    Only • Unexpected Benoa • Turtle
    Island • A Fishing Beach • Temple
    above the Stone • Surfing Mecca
Kuta   124
    Yellow Sands and Technicolor Sunsets •
    An Exotic Fairground • A Day in the
    Sun • The Sunset Event • A Meeting
    of Cultures • Lethal Rips • Kuta's
    History • Where to Stay • Where to
    Eat • Disco Fever • Shopping
South Bali: Tanah Lot to Ubud   136
    Tanah Lot • Mengwi • Sangeh •
    Ubud • Sayan
Round Central Bali   146
    Tegalalang • Tirta Empul • Gunung
    Kwai • The Moon of Pejeng • Yeh
    Pulu • Elephant Cave • Bangli
The Heights   151

Penelocan • Air Panas – Hot Spring •
The Ascent of Batur • Across the Lake •
Trunyan • Climbing Abang • Batur
and Kintamani • Penulisan • Besakih •
The Ascent of Agung • Rendang to
Klungkung • Bedugul
East Bali   166
  Klungkung • Gelgel and Kamasan •
  The Coast Road • Padangbai •
  Tenganan • Candi Dasa • Amlapura
  (Karangasem) • Water Palaces

OFF THE BEATEN TRACK   179
Nusa Penida and Nusa Lembongan   180
Nusa Penida   182
  A Limestone Island • Sampalan • A
  Cave • Peed • Across Country •
  A Cliff Stairway
Nusa Lembongan   186
  Jungutbatu
West Bali   187
  The National Park • Menjangan Island •
  Along the Coast • Buffalo Races

LASTLY . . .
THE EARTHLY PARADISE   191
  Infinity Everywhere • A Darker
  Version • The Hippie Trail •
  The Future • Moments of Vision

TRAVELERS' TIPS   197
Passports, Visas, Etc.   198
Customs Allowances   198
  Drugs

Health   199
Currency   199
From the Airport   200
Accommodation   200
Restaurants   201
Airline Offices   202
Travel Agents and Tours   202
Overland to Java   202
Transport   203
  Car Rental • Bemo Culture •
  Motorbikes
Media   204
  Television and Radio •
  Newspapers
Communications   205
  Telephone • Mail
Clothing   206
Bargaining   206
Tipping   207
Water Sports   207
  Surfing • Sailing and Windsurfing •
  Diving • Safety in Surf
Religion   208
Etiquette   208
Sex   209
Language   209
Consulates and Embassies   209
Selected Indonesian Missions Abroad   210
BIBLIOGRAPHY   212

QUICK REFERENCE A-Z GUIDE   213
To Places and Topics of Interest with Listed
Accommodation, Restaurants and Useful
Telephone Numbers

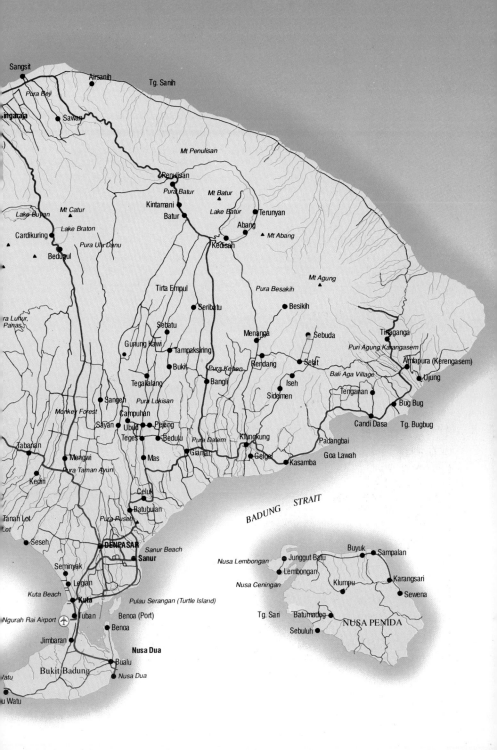

The Island of Bali

VOLCANOES IN THE OCEAN

Most modern geographers believe that Australia is slowly but unstoppably moving northward. It's nothing to worry about – reliable estimates put the speed of this movement at approximately equal to that of the growth of a human finger-nail. Nevertheless, the immense area of ocean floor surrounding the Australian landmass has, over the millennia, edged up against the sea bed extending south from mainland Asia, and, where they have made contact, been forced downwards and underneath it. Consequently, the edge of what the geologists call the Australian Plate now lies under the edge of the Asian one, and, as it nudges its way northward, it is forced deeper and deeper into the molten magma of the earth's inner mantle.

Owing to the phenomenal heat in the earth's depths, these slowly descending rocks have melted. In addition, movement on such a scale has caused unimaginable pressure to build up underground. Consequently this newly molten material has taken advantage of weaknesses in the earth's crust to burst through and surge upwards. The result has been, strung out along a line marking the meeting point of two continents, a chain of volcanoes, and subsequently of islands. These islands were for long known as the East Indies and are now called Indonesia.

To be accurate, not all the islands of this immense country that straddles the equator for 5,500 km (3,400 miles) and over three time zones are volcanic in origin. But Bali is. Virtually the entire island is made up of what its line of volcanoes past and present has pushed up above the waters of the Indian Ocean. Bali *is* its volcanoes. Two of them, Agung and Batur, have erupted this century, Batur twice. Yet despite this, Bali, like its neighbor Java, teems with people. And the reason is simple: no soil is as fertile as that produced by volcanic ash, and, with a constant supply of water for irrigation guaranteed year-round by the water-retaining volcanic uplands and craters, the island is a rice-growers' paradise.

With over 170 million people, Indonesia is the fifth most populous country on earth, after China, India, Russia and the USA. Two and a half million live on Bali. This may not seem excessive for an island 150 km (90 miles) by 80 km (50 miles), but when you consider that the mountainous interior is very thinly populated, and the arid west almost deserted inland from the

coast, and that there are no cities to speak of, this represents a considerable population density.

But then life on this favored tropical island has probably never been particularly hard. And so easy has it been for Bali's farmers to grow two crops of rice a year, there has always been time to spare for other activities. The result is Bali's celebrated dance dramas, temple festivals and generally easy-going way of life that had the early tourists from the West, back

OPPOSITE: part of the palace of the Rajah of Kerangasem (modern Amlapura), with Mount Agung behind. ABOVE: *meru* at the Ulu Danu temple, Candikuning.

in the thirties, concluding they had at last discovered the Earthly Paradise.

AN EQUABLE CLIMATE

Bali, too, is possessed of a rather benign climate. Being just on the southern edge of the true equatorial region, it does not experience the year-long rainfall that produces the rain forests you find in the Amazon, the Congo or Borneo. Instead, Bali enjoys a long dry season, very rough-

earth, these winds, wet because they have crossed the seas to the north of Indonesia, become Bali's wet season northwest monsoon. By contrast, in the Australian winter winds blow northward from the cooling continent and, coming from so dry a place across a relatively narrow ocean, become the southeasterlies of Bali's dry season.

Records show that the south of the island receives annually 78 percent of the maximum possible sunlight (and 63 percent even in January, the wettest month),

ly from April to October, and a shorter wet season, from November to March.

These seasons are caused by the relative heating and cooling of the great continents to the south and north of the Indonesian islands. In the Australian summer that continent becomes hotter than its surrounding seas. Hot air rises, and so winds are ultimately drawn in from the cooling continent of Asia to the north. Deflected sideways by the rotation of the

Rice culture – ABOVE: rice terraces near Ubud. The island's intricate terracing system, one of its many glories, is best seen in the center and east of the island. OPPOSITE: rice being brought home at harvest time.

so even during the rainy season skies are often clear for days on end. Furthermore, though it's often hot, temperatures never equal the levels they can reach in, for example, Greece or North Africa in summer. Cooling breezes attracted in from the sea by the high volcanoes ensure a climate where on the coast the average monthly temperature doesn't exceed 31°C (89°F), yet where the average monthly minimum never drops below 24°C (78°F). Day and night, wet season and dry, the temperature remains warm but equable. It's a lot cooler, and with a bigger difference between day and night, up in the mountains.

What prevents the Balinese climate being ideal is the constantly high relative humidity – 75 percent on average. This is the factor that can make temperatures that are not excessive in themselves at times extremely wearying.

TROPIC LANDSCAPE

The physical shape of Bali is simply a product of the forces that created it.

The volcanoes that form its central spine fall steeply to the sea in the north, leaving only a few valleys and a narrow coastal strip where agriculture is possible. To the south and east of the mountains, however, because the land has been lifted by the deeply burrowing edge of the Australian coastal plate, the slopes are gentler and extensive alluvial plains have been deposited. This area of very rich volcanic soils cut into by fast-flowing streams is the Balinese heartland and the site of its great kingdoms and their highly developed cultures.

The same lifting that produced lush southern Bali also raised from the sea bed the large limestone island of Nusa Penida, and the limestone peninsula south of the airport, probably also once an island, known as the Bukit.

Western Bali tapers away toward Java as the land-creating volcanoes, now it seems extinct, decrease in size.

Bali's coral reefs and silted-up estuaries have meant that the island has been without natural harbors. During the dry season the southeasterlies produce the heavy surf for which southern Bali is famous but which makes landing any kind of boat difficult, and during wet months the northwest monsoon makes access to the nearest thing Bali has to a natural harbor, Singaraja's, all but impossible. Nowadays large ships use Padangbai in the east, but even here liners have to anchor offshore and offload their passengers by lighter. Southwest Bali, however, protected by Java from the worst of the weather, is

the home of the island's largest fishing fleets.

Bali's fauna and flora are very similar to Java's. The roar of the old Balinese tiger has probably been silenced now forever, even in its last refuges in remote west Bali. Similarly, crocodiles are no longer on show in the Prancak River. Wild monkeys, though, are still common, as are various kinds of bats. Turtles are regularly caught and slaughtered for temple feasts. The domesticated Balinese pig can

be seen in every village, and so can the beautiful faun-like Balinese cattle. Water buffalo lug carts along the roads in the north.

Bali's forests consist of the spectacularly tall and skeletal coral tree, the erect and unbranching *pala*, teak, mahogany and, high on the mountains, pine. A sacred banyan tree stands somewhere in every village, and huge *kepuh* are frequently found growing round cemeteries. There are several species of palm – coconut, *lontar* (providing leaves for making traditional-style books), *sago* (providing sap for palm beer, and material for thatching) and *salak* (yielding the fruit of the same name).

The waxy white and yellow flowers of the frangipani spread their sweet scent around many a temple precinct.

FROM JAVA MAN TO GOLKAR

It's almost certain that originally man spread outwards from the tropical regions of the world, and specimens of early man have been found in Java. The basic Malay-type population of modern Indonesia appears to have been there for several thousand years at least, and the evidence of the wide extent of peoples speaking Malayo-Polynesian languages points to a large ethnic group extending from peninsular Malaysia in the west eastwards to the Philippines.

To this population, with its belief in spirits that inhabit all places and all things, came Indian Hinduism, in about the second century AD. The reason isn't hard to see.

If you want to travel from India to China, and not have to cross the highest mountain ranges on the planet, you must sail south, down the coast of Burma and through the narrow Straits of Malacca that lie between peninsular Malaysia and Sumatra. Once trade became established along this route, it cannot have been long before the desire of the Indian merchants to trade with the islands, and especially with rich Java to the south, combined with the ambitions of the Sumatrans to exert some measure of control over the trade sailing past their shores to produce extensive cultural interaction. Then the natural tendency of the more complex and more highly organized culture to dominate the simpler and less sophisticated one meant that both Indian and Chinese influences on the tropical islands south of the Asian mainland began early.

Along with Hinduism, the Indian merchants and priests brought with them their

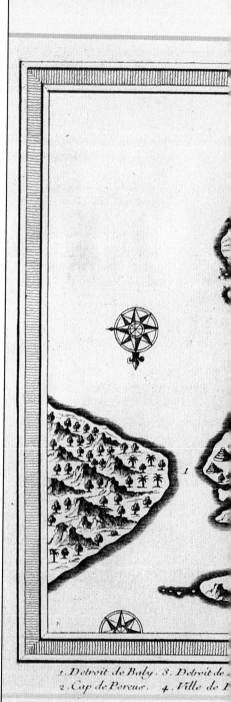

1. *Detroit de Baly* . 3. *Detroit de*
2. *Cap de Porcus* .   4. *Ville de B*

An old French map of Bali. The island is seen from the north, with Java on the right and Nusa Penida to the left. The number 4 marks Denpasar – *Ville de Baly* ("Bali town").

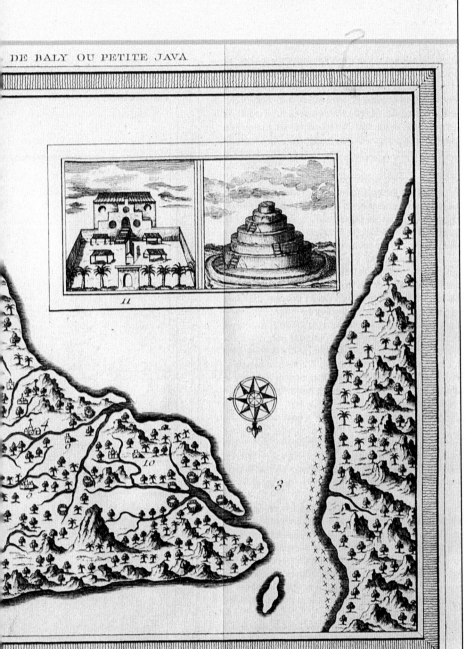

DE BALY OU PETITE JAVA.

5. Cocterius. 7. Palais du Roy. 9. Palais du Roy. 11. Plan d'un Palais du Roy.
6. Capua. 8. Coulaen. 10. Palais du Roy.

T. VIII. N.º XIII.

whole complexly interrelated culture – Sanskrit, the caste system, and Indian mythology. Remnants of all these are still found even in Moslem Java, where the shadow puppet plays and the dance dramas continue to portray the characters of the great Indian epics.

Under these influences, and with a naturally rich soil, Java eventually produced a series of powerful Hindu, and later Buddhist, civilizations, from the Mataran to the Majapahit. Sumatra, less easy to cultivate, concentrated on the control of trade, and its Srivijaya empire too flourished. At their most extensive, the maritime trade routes stretched from China to Arabia and East Africa, and all through the Straits of Malacca. Bali, rather on the edge of things, and lacking both the natural resources and harbors of Java, joined and left empires as they waxed and waned.

These old Hindu empires, with connections as far west as Madagascar, must have been something very exotic. How far their imported culture penetrated into the lives of the ordinary people is another matter. The immense Buddhist temple at Borobodur in central Java and the nearby Hindu one at Prambanan are, however, evidence both of extraordinary dedication and exceptional powers of organization.

And just as trade with India and China had brought Hindu and later Buddhist priests to Indonesia, as well as Chinese scholars, so trade with Arabia eventually led to the arrival of Islam in the archipelago.

Everywhere along the coast of Java in the fifteenth century, rajahs were becoming sultans, and the final outcome of this expansion of Islam into the region was the fall of the great Majapahit empire and the flight of its aristocracy, priesthood and community of artists and scholars across the narrow strait from east Java onto the neighboring island of Bali.

The emperor became the king of Bali and rajah of Klungkung, and the rest of the island was divided up into seven

diminutive kingdoms – Bandung, Tabanan, Bangli, Gianyar, Karangasam (Amlapura), Buleleng (Singaraja) and Jembrana (West Bali) – and given to members of the ex-Majapahit royal family to rule. Men used to ruling an empire now began to focus their attention on a medium-sized island.

These Balinese kingdoms vied with one another over the centuries, first one becoming dominant, then another. But culturally, and, more important, religiously, the island was a whole. On great festival days the Balinese traveled to the Mother Temple at Besakih irrespective of the kingdom they resided in. Though there were wars between them from time to time, it seems likely these kingdoms were largely the playthings of the rajahs who ruled them. Their boundaries form the basis for the island's modern administrative districts.

Quite why Islam never moved into Bali as well remains something of a mystery. Islam certainly extended further east into Sulawesi and the Moluccas. The root reason is probably that the faith spread with trade, and Bali, with little to offer and no harbors, was consequently ignored.

Nevertheless, this prolonged cultural interaction has left its mark on the island. There are Moslems in the eastern-facing ports of Padangbai and Kusamba, and Buddhist priests work alongside the Hindu ones. And up in the mountains, the Bali Aga, old-style Balinese who never accepted the caste system and other imports brought in with Hinduism, continue their intransigent existence.

Thus Bali (with a section of western Lombok) became what it remains today, the only predominantly non-Islamic territory in the entire archipelago, and an isolated outpost of Indian Hindu culture

---

Two Balinese men at around the turn of the century. Western influence on the East Indies began early, but Bali was largely left alone because of its lack of ports and mountainous interior.

gorgeously stranded in the tropical seas south of the equator.

And rather than fade away, cut off from its source, Balinese culture has flourished, apparently intact, and continues to do so today, even in the presence of an unprecedented influx of tourism and consequent Western materialism.

It could be argued that the Balinese were well trained in keeping foreign influences at bay by three hundred years of contact with the Dutch. Improved

suppressed, surplus clove trees (which threatened to lower prices in Europe) were burnt down, and the islands were made to grow an ever-increasing proportion of crops marketable back in Amsterdam. Cloves were sold for approximately 15 times the price paid for them. The old Arab-Chinese-Malay monopoly of the trade was at an end.

The Dutch first set foot in Bali in 1597, taking home glowing reports. Despite this aesthetic appreciation, the

ship production brought the various European powers to the East in the sixteenth century. Acquiring spices quickly became the prime object of their expeditions; these were used not only to flavor meat but, far more importantly, to preserve it. Soon cloves, cinnamon, nutmeg and the rest were fetching staggering prices in Lisbon and Amsterdam. It was the Dutch who eventually came to dominate this immensely lucrative business and, as the British were later to do in India, soon began administering the territories they were exploiting. The former trade of what became known in Europe as the East Indies was

search for profits led them to Java and the eastern spice Islands of the archipelago first and foremost and, as had happened previously, Bali was ignored. If the Balinese learned any lesson from their first contact with Europeans it was probably the dangerous one that outside influence was easily deflected. The truth was the Dutch had enough on their hands in the more profitable corners of the region. The trade in spices, it is true, ceased to be the license to print money it had been, and control of the islands was even temporarily lost to the British during the Napoleonic Wars when the French occupation of Holland was taken as an excuse for seizing all Dutch possessions in Asia as war booty. Nevertheless, the peace treaty saw the Dutch colonies returned, with minor adjustments, and interest in the region revived by the introduction of American cash crops such as cotton and tobacco into the islands.

One product Bali had traditionally been valued for was slaves. By the end of the eighteenth century up to two thousand Balinese were being shipped abroad annually into serfdom. The trade was finally abolished in 1830.

The nineteenth century, like the centuries before it, saw several revolts against Dutch rule. The most notable was the so-called Java War of 1825-30 where Javanese resistance was led by one Prince Diponegoro. Major streets in Denpasar and Klungkung are now named after him.

The first Dutch occupation was an attempt to occupy, as opposed to keep an eye on, Bali came in 1846 when the Balinese plundering of a wreck was used as a pretext for moving in and eventually controlling the northern and western districts of the island. From then on a policy of divide and rule set the remaining Balinese kingdoms against one another until one side made the tactical error of appealing to the Dutch for assistance against its neighbors. This was what the Dutch had been waiting for and they promptly annexed the kingdom they were helping, Gianyar, in 1900.

Another instance of the looting of a wreck, this time off Sanur, led to the completion of Dutch control. This, however, did not become final until after the massacre of four thousand Balinese in Denpasar where the entire aristocracy presented itself in full ceremonial dress for ritual *puputan*, or resistance to the last man, against what were clearly superior forces. This was on September 20, 1906. A similar heroic but suicidal last stand took place in Klungkung, and then it was all over and the Dutch were masters of the whole island.

Their rule was not liked. A rigid policy of white supremacy was enforced and little was done to benefit the Balinese.

The early thirties was the time when the first Western artists began arriving in Bali, men like Walter Spies, who lived in Ubud, and Miguel Covarrubias and Le Mayeur who settled near Denpasar and in Sanur respectively. They lived with, or at least alongside, the local people, and made a

point of being independent of the Dutch administrators. They were in Bali because of the idyllic existence to be had there, in which culture and an easy life seemed to go hand in hand, and they had no use for the distinctions deemed necessary by the colonial masters for the perpetuation of their system.

Well-off tourists, too, began arriving at this time despite the difficulties and expense of travel; it's estimated that about a hundred a month were visiting Bali by the middle of the decade.

OPPOSITE: Twentieth century colonists and visitors recorded in stone. ABOVE: in the temple at Kubutambahan, North Bali.

A good account of the period is K'tut Tantri's *Revolt in Paradise*. An American citizen, she settled in Bali in 1933, adopted local dress and a Balinese name, and stayed in Bali and Java until the late forties. Her book is also a good guide to the events that followed the outbreak of the Second World War.

The Japanese entered the war in 1941 and proceeded very quickly to overrun Singapore, Malaya, Burma, the Philippines and the Dutch East Indies. The Dutch colonial army finally surrendered to them on March 7, 1942. Japanese anticolonial propaganda didn't win the support of the Indonesians for long, but the opportunity was taken by some of the emerging nationalist leaders to advance their cause, and on the defeat of Japan the independent Republic of Indonesia was bravely proclaimed on August 17, 1945.

The Dutch, however, had other ideas. In association with British forces they landed in Indonesia with the ostensible purpose of disarming and interning the Japanese troops there. Before long, however, troops of both nations were fighting armed Indonesian volunteers, and in November 1945 Surabaya was shelled from the sea, and bombed, by British forces.

Eventually the British fell back on the role of go-betweens, but the guerrilla war against the Dutch continued until, on December 27, 1949, under international pressure, The Hague agreed to recognize the sovereignty of the Republic of Indonesia.

The country's first president was the long-established leader of the independence movement, Dr Sukarno (who had a Balinese mother). He held power until the combined effects of a declining economy, militant anti-Americanism, a rash "confrontation" with Malaysia and the increasing influence of the In-

Bali is extraordinary in the continuance of Hinduism there thousands of miles away from its Indian home. Processions to the temple such as this one are a reasonably common occurrence.

donesian communist party (PKI) led to an alleged coup attempt by the PKI on the night of September 30, 1965. This was swiftly outmaneuvered by the army, and since that date Major-General (now President) Suharto has been in control. Policies have been pragmatic and pro-Western, and the PKI has been declared illegal. A degree of democracy has been restored but to date the power of the ruling Golkar party has nowhere been effectively challenged, and it is they and the army who essentially control the country.

This turnabout in the nation's political orientation was not effected, however, without a terrible purge of communists, suspected communists, and, most notably, Chinese in the last months of 1965. The total number of victims has never been agreed on – and indeed the very account of this period is now the subject of what ideological debate is still permitted. In Bali alone the number of dead almost certainly exceeded a hundred thousand, and the killing there was more extensive and brutal than anywhere else in the country. According to one observer, "Whole villages, including children, took part in an island-wide witch-hunt for communists who were slashed and clubbed and chopped to death by communal consent." It's a sobering thought when considering a culture dubbed by so many as one characterized by beauty, harmony, and a serene adherence to the will of the gods.

Today Bali basks in the relative prosperity brought to it by tourism. Eighty-five percent of all Indonesia's tourists come here, and only here. For the rest, the economy remains exclusively agricultural, dominated by rice-production. The new "miracle" rice means the island now produces a surplus for export. Other exports include copra and coffee. And the Chinese are back and doing good business, in the restaurants, clothes shops and travel agencies of Kuta and elsewhere.

A Note on Language

Bali has its own language, Balinese. Though part of the Malayo-Polynesian family of languages, it's as distinct from Malay (Indonesian) as English is from German. It exists in three forms, High, Middle and Low. Lower-ranking people must use High Balinese when speaking to their superiors, but high-ranking individuals use Low Balinese when speaking to their inferiors

or amongst themselves, except in very formal situations. Middle Balinese is used in delicate social circumstances.

Bahasa Indonesia, the official national language of Indonesia and indistinguishable except in occasional words from Malay, is taught in all schools as a part of government policy. Most younger Balinese can speak it when necessary.

Lastly, the ancient Javanese tongue of Kawi is used by the priests, and as the language of the gods in the shadow puppet dramas.

OPPOSITE: The taking of offerings to the local temple is a regular part of Balinese daily life.
ABOVE: At a purification ceremony, Kuta.

The Culture of Bali

A VILLAGE UPBRINGING

BANJAR AND SUBAK

With the exception of the Bali Aga settlements, Balinese villages all follow a similar pattern.

The village is invariably on either side of a road. Along this road run thatched walls with somewhat higher roofed gateways, also thatched, leading into the family compounds. Side roads at right angles to the main road lead to the rice terraces, while immediately behind the family compounds are kitchen gardens where crops such as green vegetables and corn are grown.

Somewhere in the center of the village will stand the communal buildings, the village temple *(pura desa)*, the assembly pavilion *(bale agung)*, the *kul-kul* tower, and, more often than not, a sacred banyan tree.

Some way away from the village will be the village cemetery, a rough grassy field surrounded by trees where cremations take place and bodies are buried temporarily prior to cremation. A small temple of the dead *(pura dalem)* will also be there.

Low-bellied pigs forage freely round the village and mangy dogs hang out, despised and only half tolerated. Fighting cocks in round bamboo cages are often placed on the ground where they may be seen and admired, and where they can peck at the earth before being moved on to a new patch.

Chickens, too, wander at will, but ducks are herded daily into the rice paddies where they are kept together by means of a tall pole topped with a white cloth. For some reason the ducks never stray far from this marker.

Balinese villages are shady, well-tended places where gardens, and the communal manipulation of running water, give a strong sense of security and order.

Villages are run by a council *(krama desa)* of which every married householder is a member. This council elects one of its members as leader *(klian desa)* and meets in the *bale agung*. It orders the life of the village and makes arrangements for festivals. It can also administer punishment, essentially expulsion: this is very serious in Bali as, once expelled from his village, a man will find no refuge anywhere else on the island.

It isn't long before the visitor realizes that every hotel worker he comes into contact with identifies strongly with his village and hurries back there whenever he has a couple of days off, even if it's on the opposite side of the island.

Large villages and towns are subdivided into *banjar.* These operate just like villages, each with its own temple, council, *bale agung* and the rest. In this way, village organization continues, even in the capital Denpasar. Each *banjar* has its own festival on its temple *odalan* (anniversary – see HIGH DAYS, p.47), and, on the night before Nyepi – a great all-island festival – each *banjar* in Denpasar parades its own lovingly made monster through the central streets without any hint of rivalry.

The Balinese aristocrats still often live in their palaces *(puri)*, and these are sited within villages rather than outside them. These large walled compounds are like miniature villages in themselves, containing houses for different family members, each with its own garden and sub- dividing wall. There is no real middle class in rural Bali. The Chinese businessmen and the shopkeepers of Kuta, together with the other self-made people, tend to live in or just outside Denpasar.

Although various rice fields are nowadays owned by individual villagers, the old cooperative system of agriculture still

Rice is central to the island's life. These beautifully terraced fields have been flooded for the planting-out of the young shoots.

continues to exist. One of the reasons for this is that irrigation *has* to be communal, and the flow of the water, the careful provision of exactly the right amount of water for all the fields before it is allowed to flow away downstream to the next village, requires the most careful and intricate management.

The organizations that oversee this operation are known as *subak*. Everyone who owns a rice field is a member. The *subak* meets monthly, sometimes more often, at the shrine out in the rice field dedicated to the deities of agriculture. Decisions are then made as to what repairs or improvements are needed, and who shall be responsible for carrying them out.

THE CULT OF RICE

To the Balinese, to eat is to eat rice. As elsewhere in Indonesia – which indicates the cult is pre-Hindu – the rice plant is treated as a woman, and the stages of her birth, growth, pregnancy and final fruition are all celebrated. She is Dewi Sri, the rice goddess.

First comes the laying out of the seed to germinate. This is considered worthy of a small offering and done on a propitious date by the Balinese calendars. Some 45 days later the shoots are planted out in the waterlogged paddies, first in a ritual pattern – nine seedlings in the shape of a star – then in rows one hand-span apart. Nowadays, however, such ceremonies are usually preceded by an application of trisodium phosphate, a government-recommended fertilizer.

Forty-two days later her "birthday" is celebrated with altars in the fields. When the grain first appears, Dewi Sri is said to be with child. Altars are again erected in the fields and foods that pregnant women

ABOVE: Weeding between the growing rice plants; note the low banks between fields and the subtly-varied water levels. Such terraces are maintained, and the water flow controlled, by close cooperation between and within villages. Competition would be unthinkable. OPPOSITE: Rice shoots waiting to be planted.

have a taste for are presented as offerings. Rites are performed to ward off the vermin (or evil spirits) that might attack the grain.

Four months after the planting out (five months for traditional strains) comes the harvest. Effigies are made of Dewi Sri and her husband Wisnu from the first sheaves and taken to the cultivator's household temple. A Rice Mother is made and placed to oversee the harvest to the end.

The ingenuous look on the face of the little Dewi Sri figures called *cili* can often be seen in Balinese art, and in unexpected places everywhere. With their primordial simplicity, *cili* represent the impish soul of the island.

Only men plant and tend the rice, but everyone takes part in the harvest. It's a collective activity, too, and the harvesters go from one irrigation cooperative to another till the work is over.

The rice cultivated in Bali is nowadays almost exclusively the new "miracle" rice, a shorter, less elegant plant than the old rice depicted in paintings from before the seventies, but yielding at least a 50 percent larger crop, and over a shorter growing period. The older kind, however, is said to taste better and fetches a higher price than the "miracle" variety in the markets.

WHERE DO YOU SIT?

Caste is almost certainly more deeply embedded in the Balinese psyche than appears at first sight.

In the same way that the Hindu religion was brought, in the Majapahit invasion, to

Some commentators have judged that caste in modern Bali represents little more than a pleasant diversion. Perhaps this is the impression the Sudras would like to give, and that the top-dog Brahmanas can afford to give (seeing as they are often also the richest people around). Nevertheless, the complexities of an intercaste marriage have not lessened with the arrival of a few hundred thousand tourists on the beaches of Kuta and Sanur.

a people previously content with worshipping spirits of place and of their ancestors, so too the age-old Hindu distinction between people born to different roles in life was superimposed on a culture that was essentially collective and probably relatively classless. And just as the Balinese have taken to the one, so they have accepted the other. Despite the fact that 93 percent of the population has to be content with membership of the lowest of the four castes, the Sudra, they appear to accept uncritically the claims of the other three castes, and even at times, when away from their home villages, seek to adopt their status for themselves.

Essentially, the Brahmanas were the priestly caste, the Satrias the warriors, the Wesias the merchants, and the Sudras the ordinary people. A long-standing struggle between the Brahmanas and the Satrias over which of them was the senior group seems to have been resolved in a de facto victory for the Brahmanas.

The following titles are used by the four groups as prefixes to their names:

Brahmana Men: Ida Bagus; women: Ida Ayu (Dayu for short). Both these mean "high-born and beautiful."

Satrias Men: Cokorde, Anak Agung, Ratu, Prebagus; women: Anak Agung Isti, Dewa Ayu.

Wesia Men: I Gusti, Pregusti; Women: I Gusti Ayu.

Sudra Men: I; women: Ni.

Legally, feudal discrimination according to caste is forbidden. And it is true that Brahmanas can be found waiting at table in restaurants and Sudras occupying reasonably important government positions. Nevertheless, socially the habits of deference persist, and "Where do you sit?" (referring to the custom of always sitting lower than someone of a higher caste) remains a question strangers will sooner or later ask each other on first acquaintance.

NAMING OF NAMES

Balinese personal names usually refer to the position of the child in the family order. The first-born is Wayan – or, in the higher castes, Putu or Gede. The second is Made – or Nengah or Kadek. The usual name for the third-born is Nyoman, with Komang as an alternative. The fourth child is Ketut. These names are used for boys and girls indiscriminately. After four, the cycle is repeated, with the fifth child Wayan again and so on.

SEX ROLES

Distinction according to sex is more rigorous than that according to class.

Only men work as craftsmen (weaving excepted), climb coconut trees, tend cattle or cultivate the fields (though women invariably help with the rice harvest). And only women do the housework, look after the chickens and pigs, and prepare offerings for temples.

What most surprises Westerners is to see women doing all the heavy labor on construction sites and on roadworks. The principle here is that whereas it's the men who build the traditional Balinese wooden

Threshing rice in North Bali. Everyone takes part in a scene that can be seen at any time of year as the climate allows crops to be planted and harvested more or less at will.

houses, the women do the dirty work in Western-style building.

Also, it is the custom for women to carry goods on their heads, men to carry them slung at either end of a pole they carry on their shoulders. It's normally women who carry offerings to the temple, but when a man does this he too must carry them on his head.

Nevertheless, Balinese women do enjoy a measure of independence by Asian standards, keeping the profits from their economic activities for themselves and also easily obtaining a divorce from an unsatisfactory husband without incurring any very serious social disapproval.

BIRTH, CHILDHOOD, LOVE AND MARRIAGE

There are few guidebooks that fail to point out that family life is particularly important to the population under discussion. Nevertheless, it does seem to be genuinely the case with the Balinese. The existence of offspring to ensure you have an adequate cremation is essential, and the more children there are to bear the cost of this expensive ceremony the better. In earlier times, and possibly still, Western contraception devices were considered akin to black magic. Failure to bear children is an acceptable ground for divorce (as is male impotence) in Balinese society.

Three months into pregnancy the mother-to-be is subject to a ceremony, and during the whole gestation period she will probably wear one or more amulets to protect her from the attention of *leyak* (witches) anxious to feed on the entrails of the unborn child. After the birth itself, the mother is considered unclean *(sebel)* for 42 days (and the father for three days).

In a bizarre belief, the newborn child is considered to be accompanied by four "brothers" ("sisters" in the case of a girl),

Girl taking an offering to the temple. Under a very free system of child-rearing, the Balinese mature early and retain a natural dignity throughout adult life.

the *kanda empat*. These have their physical manifestation in the placenta, blood, skin-coating and amniotic fluid, all of which are saved and buried with great solemnity, the place being marked with a shrine.

It's a sign of the unequal effects of inherited beliefs on the Balinese that not so long ago the birth of twins of the opposite sex was considered as a disaster by the ordinary people, necessitating, among other things, the removal and eventual destruction of the family's house and the impoverishment of the father of the ill-begotten unfortunates. Among the upper castes, however, the twins were considered the reincarnations of two souls previously happily married, and their birth the occasion for great rejoicing. The situation probably represented the continuance of ancient Balinese beliefs among the ordinary people and the more successful dissemination of Hindu ideas among the upper classes, many of whom descended en masse on Bali in the sixteenth century from Java.

After 14 days, the newborn child is named, but it's only after 105 days (three months of 35 days each) that the child is allowed to touch the ground for the first time, the occasion being marked, not unexpectedly, with a ceremony. Another similar ceremony takes place after one complete Balinese year (210 days – see TIME PASSES BY, p. 43) and in practice the two ceremonies are frequently combined on the later date to reduce the expense of the necessary feasting of guests and hiring of priests.

The Balinese allow their children to live an unusually natural life, as if carefully following the precepts of the most advanced child psychologists. They are suckled for as long as they want, often over three years, and allowed to feed – just like their parents – whenever they're hungry. They are held in permanent bodily contact with either the mother or another woman of the family for every moment of the first three months of life, and throughout early

Balinese children enjoy in their earliest years.

The relaxed attitude to sex goes on to apply to marriage. Parents have a minimal part to play in the arrangements, and in the commonest form of marriage the ceremony doesn't take place until several days after the announcement of consummation. And even in upper-caste "arranged" marriages, the couple may sleep

childhood fathers cuddle or carry their children almost as often as their mothers. Not surprisingly, Balinese children rarely cry.

Once they're able to walk, the children live a free and easy life in the village in the company of other children of their own age. They are never beaten, and little in adult life is hidden from them so that they appear to enter the world of sex at adolescence without surprise, guilt or neurosis.

Sexual relations between Balinese teenagers are left to proceed in a natural way without interference from the parents, at least in the Sudra class that makes up the vast majority of the population, and there's no expectation that early affairs will necessarily lead to marriage. Love charms and magically potent amulets are often used where the girl seems reluctant. Homosexuality is frowned on but seems anyway rare, possibly as a result of the relaxed sensual life

together for an agreed period before the wedding.

The commonest form of marriage in Bali is by kidnaping *(ngrorod)*. The boy seizes the girl in some public place and, after token resistance, the couple speed off to a prearranged hidey-hole where offerings are set out for the gods and the union hurriedly consummated. It's considered vital this happens before the offerings wilt in order for the union to be valid. This is the real marriage, performed in the sight of the gods, and the subsequent public celebration is merely a recognition of an already-achieved actuality.

Arranged marriages *(mapadik)* are commonest among the aristocracy, but only with the full agreement of both boy and girl.

The charm of the Balinese is the charm of a people whose natural grace has been sustained and augmented by a religion that is based on respect and reverence for the life of all things.

The wedding ceremonies take place at the home of the boy's father. A tooth-filing ritual (see next entry) will be incorporated if this operation hasn't been performed already. There's much feasting and music, but the actual ceremony is a simple one with the priest just blessing the union amid much throwing of flowers, ringing of bells and dashing with holy water.

A Balinese woman couldn't in the past normally marry a man of lower caste than herself, a prohibition that merely echoed the attempts of the rich everywhere to try to make sure their daughters don't descend the social scale when they marry. If this is changing nowadays, it's changing slowly. Mar-

riage with divorcees and widows, however, is freely allowed.

Balinese women can divorce their husbands – for cruelty, impotence or failure to support them – by simply walking out of the house. The divorce is then confirmed by the village council; this is generally a formality as there are no set criteria by which "support" or "cruelty" can be judged.

TOOTH-FILING

It is considered essential for every Balinese adult sooner or later to have his teeth filed – so much so that in the event of accidental death in youth the teeth of the body will be filed before cremation.

The purpose of the ceremony is to reduce the power of the vices of greed, jealousy, anger, drunkenness, lust and "confusion" that are considered more appropriate to animals than to humans. Consequently, the two upper canine teeth, and the four incisors between them, are filed down amid feasting and general celebration. Because of the cost of the hospitality involved, tooth-filing ceremonies are often held in conjunction with other rituals. And because it's thought desirable to have had your teeth filed before you get married, the ceremony is frequently held in conjunction with a wedding.

Ideally, the six teeth are filed down by someone of the Brahmana cast Perhaps the upper-caste patron of the family

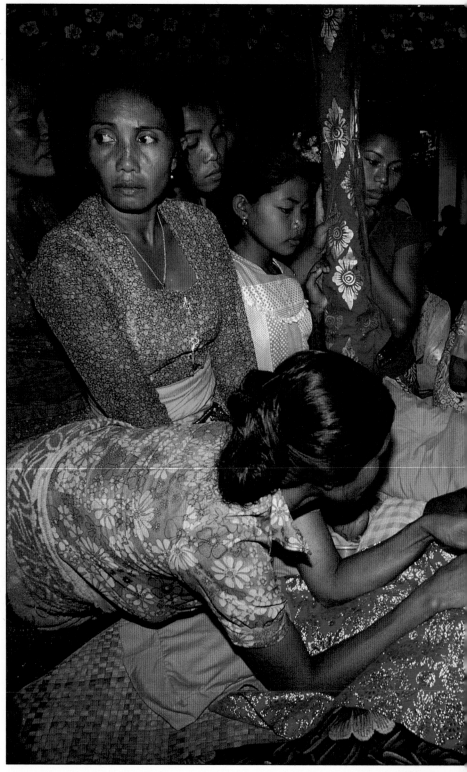

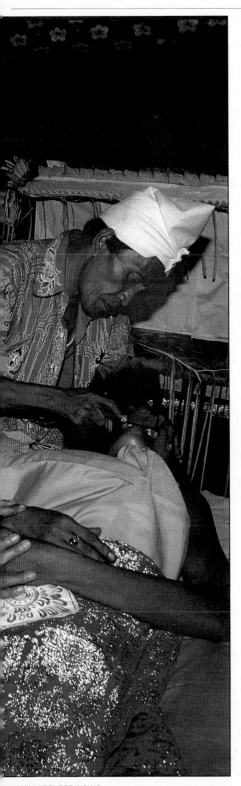

concerned. The patients, dressed in their finest, lie down in a pavilion, usually two at a time, surrounded by offerings. They are then wrapped in a white cloth while family and friends gather round.

The extent to which the teeth are filed down depends largely on the wishes of the subject, but as filed teeth are considered beautiful as well as an aid to virtue, it's not uncommon for a thorough job to be requested. The filing usually takes between 15 and 30 minutes. The mouth is held open

by a short piece of sugar-cane and from time to time the patient spits out the filings into a yellow coconut which is later buried in the family temple. A small mirror allows the victim to inspect the work and request improvements. Often hundreds of young men and women have their teeth filed together in one ceremony to save on expense.

Tooth-filing – this curious custom is still rigorously observed by all Balinese, and no young man or woman can be married before the ceremony has been completed. Groups of adolescents often have their teeth filed together, and marriage and tooth-filing rituals frequently take place together.

MEN AND GODS

BALINESE HINDUISM

Every Balinese will describe himself to you as a Hindu, but the truth of the matter is that the elements of Hinduism found in Bali are rather like the Catholicism found in the remoter parts of the Philippines. For some it may be a genuine presence, and its philosophy a real foundation for faith and action, but for the majority it is a dressing applied to the more fundamental and essential spirit-religion found everywhere in the Malay archipelago.

Nevertheless, it is an extraordinary phenomenon to find, isolated on one south-sea island, manifestations of a religion originating somewhere near the Caspian Sea and brought into north India nearly four thousand years ago. Even then the tenets of Hinduism were far from new. The origins of the Vedas, the holy books of the Aryans who brought Hinduism to India, are lost in the mists of antiquity, but the oldest of them, the Rig Veda, is certainly the oldest religious text known anywhere in the world.

And the central tenets of Hinduism do fit in very well with a system of beliefs that holds that the world is everywhere populated by spirits. A people who believed from the start that in every bush, volcano, fortunate or disastrous event there was an invisible intelligence at work cannot have found it difficult to take to a philosophy that taught of a World Soul of which we, and all other living things, are temporary embodiments.

To the educated Hindu, the whole universe is ordered by a controlling spirit, Brahman. Your inner essence, the silent core of your being that remains when all the lusts for money, sex and power are stilled, is your Atman. And the innermost secret, the core of the mystery, is that the two, your "soul" and the vast spirit of the universe, are one and the same thing. You are a part of it, manifested for a brief time in matter. So is a mouse, a tree, a grain of corn.

The cycle of birth and death, creation and destruction, goes on forever, the essence of all things constantly embodying itself in matter. And in just the same way that all things are part of the great World Spirit, so their death is no tragedy, merely the returning of the part to the whole, a whole from which innumerable new manifestations will be born.

This constant rebirth of the spirit, at a higher or lower level of creation according to the place your acts have brought you to in your last incarnation, is natural and inevitable. But it's wearisome to the high-aspiring soul who longs for permanent rest, for final union with the creating spirit itself. And because the spirits of all things and the great universal spirit are essentially one and the same, this ultimate union, or reunification, is possible. Reject all desire, which holds you down among the world of material things, and you might attain that final fusion with the ineffable and unimaginable that is known as *moksa*. You at last realize the potential that has been in you all along and become one with Brahman.

No philosophy could be more remote from Western materialism where competitiveness, greed, and the desire to conquer nature (rather than realize one's true part in it) are implied in the cult of individualism and the right, above all, to "be yourself."

This is the philosophic heart of Hinduism and, over the millennia, innumerable less pure manifestations of it have grown up in India and elsewhere, just as Christianity has seen the veneration of relics and the endless matching of texts from the Bible. So, in Bali, orientation of temples toward the volcanoes and the use of cock's blood (obtained at cockfights) in temple rituals seem remote from the pure spirituality of the Chandogya

Traditional life goes on even in the midst of the tourist invasion – a purification ceremony at Kuta. (See also next page).

Upanishad. People everywhere seem to need to see and touch, to develop local sanctities and hold on to the practices of their ancestors. But the heart of the matter lies elsewhere.

Even so, the influence of the great Hindu vision is remarkably pervasive. Balinese cremations really are genuinely cheerful affairs, and the numerous rituals preceding them and symbolizing the cutting off of attachment to the soul of the dead man or woman are living parts of or-

dinary village life. The soul must be allowed to go free, and not be held back by grief – so teaches the religion; and the result is, remarkable as it may seem, the ordinary Balinese at a cremation do not mourn. Despite all the animist belief in spirits and blood sacrifice, the essence of Indian Hinduism has entered into the people's souls.

Nevertheless, the variety of religious practice, the number of places and things that can be venerated, is astonishing. There's hardly a field, a large tree, a shop or even a discotheque on the island that doesn't have its incense-burning shrine. The same is true, it might be argued, of Hong Kong or Bangkok, but in Bali the constant attention to these household shrines, and the frequency and elaborateness of the various temple festivals, are unparalleled anywhere.

Every village *(desa)* has its temple of origin *(pura puseh)*, its temple of the dead *(pura dalem)*, its temple for the irrigation system *(pura subak)*, and any number of temples and shrines dedicated to local streams, lakes, springs, hills and waterfalls. All these must have their offerings on their holy days. In addition, evil spirits, thought to occupy their own special sites, but especially crossroads, must be placated with offerings too, thrown down casually and quickly crushed by the first passing car (but not before the greedy spirits have wolfed up their meager essence).

Thus the spirits of goodness are constantly being invited down into the world

Purification ceremony on Kuta Beach. ABOVE: A *pemangku* distributes holy water; RIGHT: facing the ocean, the devotees venerate a temporary bamboo shrine. Such ceremonies take place after, for example, a cremation.

MEN AND GODS

of everyday life, and feted at festivals, and the evil spirits kept at bay by what amount to derisory, but regular, bribes.

To the Balinese, the volcanoes are the seat of the gods. Every structure in Bali is to some extent influenced by this sense of "to the mountains" *(kaja)* being pure and the opposite direction *(kelod)* being impure. So, a house will have its shrine in its most *kaja* corner, and its pig-pen and garbage tip in its most *kelod*.

The principal festival of any temple is its anniversary *(odalan)*, occurring every 210 days from the date of its founding. Then bamboo altars and tables are put up, and offerings of fruit, cakes and flowers, piled high on the heads of the women, are brought from the nearby houses. The *pemangku* receives them, pours holy water onto the hands of the villagers and places grains of rice on their temples and brow. The villagers take flower blossoms and, holding them between the tips of their

This doesn't mean that to the Balinese the sea is impure, though some Western writers have inferred this. It is true the Balinese historically have not been sea-farers, but the sea itself is seen as a purifying element, used for cleansing symbolic items from the temple *(arca)* and one source of holy water.

These mountain-oriented temples of Bali often have a deserted, even shabby look. They contain no idols, and no priests are in attendance. Only the temple keeper *(pe-mangku)* is usually somewhere around, dressed in white, to keep the place tidy and accept the donations of visitors. On festival days, though, things are very different.

fingers, raise them to their foreheads three times before throwing them toward the shrines.

The high caste priests *(pedanda)* are said to be the direct descendants of the Indian brahmins who officiated in the old courts of Java. They only attend temple ceremonies on the most important occasions, such as aristocratic weddings, at which they sit on a high platform ringing their bells and reciting their mantras. They can be either Buddhist or Hindu *(pedanda bodda* or *pedanda siwa)*, the former going bare-headed with long hair, the latter wearing a gold and red miter crowned with a crystal ball. The chief use of these learned *pedanda* as far as the ordinary people are concerned is to make the holy water used in all temple ceremonies.

At these temple anniversary festivals male and female figures, the *arca*, made of sandalwood, or of old Chinese coins (*kepeng*), are deemed to symbolize the gods and are taken during the day to a river or the sea and symbolically washed. In addition, cockfights are sometimes

HOTELS FOR THE GODS

Walk into any Balinese temple and you'll find the same mixture of diversity and similarity you find in Christian churches. A typical Balinese temple might present itself to you as follows.

You pass from the street into the first, or outer, compound through two carved stone structures, the inside (facing) walls of which, however, have been left smooth.

staged in the afternoon. *Gamelan* orchestras play, and dance dramas may be performed. As the evening wears on, coffee and cake are offered to everyone present, and certain villagers will go into a trance (during which they may also perform a sword dance) and a spirit, it is believed, will speak through them and report on how the offerings have been received by the gods.

At dawn, the women will dance in honor of the rising sun and the elaborate offerings, their essence judged to have been devoured by the gods, will be taken back home and eventually eaten by the weary devotees.

The general effect is of a structure, tapering upwards, that has been split down the middle. This split gateway is known as a *candi bentar*.

This first compound is spacious and rather empty. It does, however, contain a white-clad *pemangku* who asks you to sign a visitors' book and pay a donation of a couple of hundred rupiahs.

The compound does contain some ordinary-looking pavilions (roofs resting on four posts, with a waist-level floor) and a brick tower. Climb the tower and you will find hanging at the top some hollowed out tree trunks with slits cut into them: these are *kul-kul*, and they are hammered in times of emergency to call the villagers into the temple compound. The pavilions are used by the *gamelan* orchestras, and for preparing offerings and cooking food, on festival days.

In this (non-existent) temple, there is no second outer compound, but if there were it would simply contain further pavilions.

At the top end of this outer court, straight in the direction of the mountains, there is a wall with a door in it. The surrounds of the door are very ornate, and the door itself intricately carved. It's called the *padu raksa*. The door stands half open, so you climb the few steps up to it and walk through. You can't go straight ahead, however, as a short wall, an *aling-aling*, bars your way. It's actually meant to bar the way of evil spirits which are thought to travel in straight lines, as well as to be rather stupid – seeing their way barred, it's hoped, they'll reverse direction and fly back out again. You, however, turn left or right and go down the steps into the inner courtyard. You are now in the holiest part of the temple.

There are a considerable number of shrines along the eastern and northern walls here. (You are in south Bali – in north Bali they'd be on the eastern and southern sides, in order to be facing the mountains.) Some of these shrines are small structures a couple of meters high, little more than high-level tables with roofs of black thatch (*ijuk*). Others, though, are high towers with multiple roofs. These are known as *meru*, and the roofs are always of an odd number. The number signifies which deity they are dedicated to, as follows: 3 – Dewi Sri (rice goddess), 5 – Isawa (one of Siwa's reincarnations), 7 – Brahma, 9 – Wisnu, 11 – Siwa. The finest *meru* in Bali can be seen at Besakih and Mengwi.

Close to the eastern wall there is a rather sounder structure with locked doors. This is the *gedong pesimpanan* and contains various dusty items – masks for *barong* dances, for instance – communally owned by the villagers and occasionally used in festivals.

Situated in the corner between north (in this case) and east is a stone throne placed at the summit of an elaborately carved stone structure. This is the *padmasana*, the chair for Ida Sanghyang Widhi Wasa, the supreme deity in the Balinese pantheon. The support for the chair is carved to represent the world as imagined in Balinese mythology, mountains supported by a turtle entwined with snakes. When there are three chairs instead of one, they are for the godhead in the form of the trinity Siwa, Wisnu and Brahma.

TIME PASSES BY

The Balinese make use of three independent calendars, a traditional Javanese calendar based on 210-day cycles, an ancient South Indian lunar calendar, and the Western – and now international – Gregorian calendar.

The old Java calendar is the basis for the calculation of the dates of all temple anniversary festivals, all of which consequently recur every 210 days. This period of time is made up of thirty weeks of seven days each – but also, superimposed on them, a whole string of other "weeks" of one, two, three, four, five, six, eight, nine and ten days each. As not all these numbers multiply exactly to 210, various extra days of the week of the four-, eight- and nine-day weeks are discreetly added at fixed points in the cycle so that all the weeks can come to an end together on the 210th day.

The result of this system is that any particular day has ten different day-of-the-week names. In practice, however, it is only the three-, five- and seven-day weeks that interest the Balinese. These, though, are very important, and special coincidences between their cycles are used as auspicious days for ceremonies and rituals. For instance, when the third day of the three-day week coincides

The festival of Kuningan, observed ten days after Galungan. These great occasions come round every 210 days and are observed all over Bali; but scarcely a day passes without a festival of some kind somewhere on the island.

with the fifth day of the five-day week, it's a good day for just about anything.

Used in conjunction with this calendar (called, by the way, *pawukon*) is the lunar system known as the *saka* calendar. Being based on the moon, this calendar features months, *sasih*, each of thirty days. Each month is deemed to begin on the day following the first appearance of the new moon *(tilem)*. Halfway through each month, of course, is the full moon, *purnama*. The 12 months are named after

the Sanskrit words for one to ten, with names derived from other sources for the last two.

The innumerable possibilities offered by the combinations of these two systems are not lost on the Balinese, and the inter-chiming of these celestial rhythms is no doubt as much a manifestation of serious play, of variations within an overall unity, as the shifting rhythms and sudden harmonies of the *gamelan* orchestra. Life to the Balinese, at least in theory, is in large

The phenomenon of "possession" – men going into a trance during a temple festival. While they are "possessed". they can endure extremes of pain without apparent ill effects.

part the observing of earthly rhythms, and harmonies that reflect imagined – and possibly actual – heavenly ones.

HIGH DAYS

The commonest as well as the most important temple festivals are the ones that celebrate the *odalan* or anniversary of the temple. The majority of these are calculated according to the *pawukon* calendar (see TIME PASSES BY) which operates on a cycle of 210 days. Below are the dates of the first day of the *pawukon* cycle up to the end of the century:

April 24, 1988
November 20, 1988
June 18, 1989
January 14, 1990
August 12, 1990
March 10, 1991
October 6, 1991
May 3, 1992
November 29, 1992
June 27, 1993
January 23, 1994
August 21,1994
March 19, 1995
October 15, 1995
May 12, 1996
December 8, 1996
July 6, 1997
February 1, 1998
August 30, 1998
March 28, 1999
October 24, 1999

The festival days of a few of the major temples of Bali are listed below. The number before the temple name indicates the day in the *pawukon* calendar on which its festival occurs. Thus Bangli's Pura Kehen, having the number four, will have its festival in 1997 on July 9, the fourth day of the *pawukon* cycle which begins in that year on July 6.

4 – Pura Kehen, Bangli.

59 – Pura Ulun Danau, Chandikuning (Bedugul).

60 – Pura Bukit Sari, Sangeh (Monkey Forest).

84 – Pura Taman Pule, Mas (three-day *odalan*).

85 – Pura Sakenan, Serangan (Turtle Island).

88 – Pura Tanah Lot.

94 – Pura Taman Ayun, Mengwi (three-day *odalan*).

94 – Pura Luhur, Uluwatu.

Certain major temple festivals are fixed according to the lunar, *saka*, calendar. All the following are held at full moon, *purnama*, in one of the two months indicated – to find out which one the year you're there, contact the Badung Tourist Office.

February/March – Pura Penataran Sasih, Pejeng.

March/April – Pura Batu, Kintamani.

March/April – Pura Besakih.

September/October – Pura Panataran Agung, Besakih.

September/October – Pura Tirtha Empul, Tampaksiring.

October/November – Pura Kehen, Bangli.

October/November – Pura Jagat Nartha, Denpasar (the state temple next to the museum).

The Badung Government Tourist Office in Denpasar publishes every month a list of imminent temple festivals, large and small, throughout the island.

THREE FESTIVALS

Nyepi celebrates the solar New Year for Bali. Despite Bali's being in the southern hemisphere, it's a sort of spring clearing-out of bad spirits. On the day before Nyepi, evil spirits are attracted down with special offerings, then terrified out of their wits as night falls by a veritable orgy of firecrackers dropped in garbage cans, gongs, beating of *kul-kul,* yelling and the parading through the streets of gigantic, hideously grotesque monsters. It's a great night to be in the streets of Denpasar and shouldn't on any account be missed.

Entrance of the *rangda* mask for a temple dance. Almost all Bali's dances are religious in origin, the only exceptions being those evolved in modern times for the benefit of foreign visitors to the island.

The next day, Nyepi itself, the entire island stays home. Even tourists aren't allowed onto the beaches, or indeed out of their hotels. It's very strictly observed, and after dark bands of vigilantes throw stones through any window where a light is visible.

The idea behind it all is, however, charmingly innocent. Most of the evil spirits having been driven out the night before, on Nyepi itself a show is made of the island being totally uninhabited. It's

the Holy Spring at the temple of Tirta Empul at Tampaksiring, the *odalan* or anniversary festival of which is on the same day. The day after Kuningan there is a festival on Turtle Island (Serangan).

A VILLAGE CREMATION

It's a hot morning. A tour organizer wakes you early and you set off, down a road, then another, down a lane, down a track and you're there.

hoped all remaining spirits will give up and fly off somewhere more congenial.

Galungan, and the festival which follows it ten days later, **Kuningan**, are celebrated every 210 days, like the temple anniversary festivals, and so can occur at any time of the year. Galungan is the time when the spirits of the ancestors return and revisit the homes of their offspring. *Barong* (giant monsters in masks) roam the streets and everything is brushed clean, dance dramas of great length are performed, and a party atmosphere prevails everywhere.

Kuningan, by contrast, is a festival of purification and is closely associated with

A high bamboo tower and a bamboo bull, richly adorned and shining in the early morning light, are standing ready in an open space in the middle of a village. Under a blue and orange canopy, the special cremation *gamelan*, the *gambong*, is already playing its old-style instruments, bamboo-keyed and struck by players holding four hammers apiece. You engage a young man in conversation.

The dead man was his grandfather. Aged sixty, he'd died 12 days ago in the hospital. They'd waited for an auspicious date for the cremation – there are maybe two in a month. This cremation, together with the ceremonies beforehand, will cost the family

US$3,000; they'd had to feed the whole village since the day of his death.

An elegantly dressed man comes out from the nearby lodgings. He's wearing sarong, waistband, headdress and tennis shoes. He photographs the bull and, by means of an attached string, tweaks its extremely virile phallus. Great laughter from the *gambong* players. He proceeds to photograph the various groups of villagers present. The tower *(wadah)* can have anything from one to eleven roofs, like the temple *meru*. This has seven. The number, always odd, depends on the caste of the deceased (see p. 41).

Everyone is dressed in their best, even "Kuta Beach" T-shirts so long as they're neat and new-looking.

The bull is moved forward, and a bamboo ramp placed against the tower. Young men in white headbands do the work. The *gambong* music becomes more excited. Women go up the ramp and rub their hair on the bier.

A procession of women carrying offerings on their heads leaves the lodgings and lines up in front of the bull. Little waves to friends in the crowd. Then they process off down the track to the intersection with the lane.

The music gets more frantic as the young men go into the lodgings; the *gambong*, previously playing in two sections, is now playing together. The odd cigarette is being smoked. One well-dressed woman comes out of the lodging carrying a plastic shopping-bag and takes up a position by the musicians.

Expectant silence now from the *gambong*. Smiles in the sunlight. Some laughter.

Two live chicks are brought out from the lodging and placed in the tower – then a long white cloth is unwound from the lodging doorway to the ramp, followed by some sausage-like bundles. The music has now resumed and is vigorous and strong.

The bull is lifted off the ground and sets off on the shoulders of the youths.

There's some argument, then it's turned round and bounced up and down. Someone has the job of jigging the genitals with the string.

Suddenly the body emerges. It's wrapped in white at the end of the sheet, and it's bundled quickly into the tower, just under the lowest roof. The *gambong* is now ringing out as the cloth is wound up and stuffed into the tower at great speed.

Away down the track, at the junction with the lane, the bull is being rather

wildly bounced and circled around. The body is tied securely into the tower with string. A man climbs onto the tower carrying a bird on a stick. The ramp's removed.

Bearers lift the tower, and immediately run round and round in a circle with it, laughing as they go.

And off you go, with the musicians carrying cymbals, gongs and drums walking

Cremations can take place in the most public places – OPPOSITE and ABOVE: a simple cremation on the beach at Sanur. A cremation in Bali is a comparatively joyful occasion as the spirit of the dead person is being released from earthly ties and becomes free to reincarnate into a higher form of existence.

in front of the tower. Down the track and left into the lane. Everyone follows, the old men with the little children (the young men are all assisting at the ceremony). The sun goes in.

You pass along the lane, past paddy fields reflecting the now dull sky. School children dressed in white are formally lined up with their teachers to witness the event. Great red flowers like gladioli glow in the hedgerows. Several immobilized motorcyclists wait on the verge for you to pass. People chat quietly among themselves as you walk along.

Tourists walk with the villagers. No one seems to mind them being there – if anything, they seem honored.

Finally you are there, and the tower is rushed into the rough field surrounded by high trees that is the burial and cremation place. The man on the tower throws grain on anybody within range. The tower's set down, and the ramp moved up to it.

The two chicks are untied, chirruping wildly. There's much argument as the body's half moved out and the white cloth unwound.

Clearly this is a much-used site. Burned straw lies around, and little bamboo shrines stand precariously. The *gambong* sets up, and strikes up again.

The body of the bull – a tree trunk with a lid cut into it – is opened up to receive the corpse, which is brought across and placed on top of the bull, supported on bamboo poles. The musicians stop playing. All but the last strips of stained cloth are removed. A sour aroma drifts across the grass. The bamboo poles are removed and the body slowly lowered into the wooden sarcophagus.

The "Village Cremation" described in the text. These days the fire is largely kerosene sprayed onto the bier from a portable tank. The actual cremation takes place at a "burning ground" just outside the village.

A lengthy wait now as the family and a priest sprinkle holy water and place items inside the bull. The people wait, chatting quietly and smoking their clove cigarettes. A drink seller toots his bicycle horn. It's like an English village fete, sociable, and pleasant and relaxed. This final placing-in of offerings is rather drawn-out. The penultimate, in life as in art, is always long.

Finally the cloth goes in, the *gambong* strikes up, and the lid is replaced in the bull's back. Plastic tubes are unwound, attached to blackened metal burners.

But the lid's removed again. The contents of the bull are checked, and a woman's making a point. Then everything's replaced and the lid put back on. The burners are put underneath and the taps opened. Kerosene (paraffin) begins to spring onto the bull and is lit by a match.

The burning is strangely non-ritualized, a technical problem. The *gambong* doesn't play. The work is done by two men in yellow plastic safety helmets.

The fire spits and roars. The body shifts position. There are explosions, bones cracking. The cloths are now burnt and the dead man grimly visible. The people are very quiet.

Then suddenly the musicians start up again, lively and even cheerful. The people relax, and your tour driver comes across and says it's time to be off.

What about the ceremony by the sea? Tomorrow. And the burning of the tower? Also tomorrow (actually later that day, but the driver wants his lunch).

And that was it.

How It Is

Bodies are often buried for some considerable time before what's left of them is exhumed for cremation. If a Balinese dies far from home, or at sea, an effigy is usually burnt in the village cemetery as a better-than-nothing substitution for the cremation proper.

The bamboo *wadah* is decorated with colored paper, tinsel, cotton ornaments and small mirrors. Sudras are entitled to only one roof, but are usually cremated in large groups, victims of the cut-price even in death. Three to eleven are reserved for the three senior castes, while a brahmanic priest or priestess has no roof at all but an empty chair akin to a temple *padmasana*. The tower and the bull are rotated frequently, and especially at crossroads, both to deceive the evil spirits and to prevent the soul of the deceased finding its way back home again. The giant head on the back of the more splendid towers is called a *bhoma*, a fanged monster with wings outstretched, decorated in colored cotton.

In the case of high-caste cremations – the kind that visitors to Bali are almost invariably taken to – there will be elaborate ceremonies too on the previous day. A procession bearing effigies *(adegan)* of the deceased will go to the house of the high priest to receive his blessing. There will be *baris* dances (see DANCE AND DRAMA, p. 64) and singing in Sanskrit, together with various small ceremonies in which members of the family symbolize their breaking of emotional ties with the dead man, ties that might otherwise hold him back in this world and keep his soul from the freedom it so desires.

In the evening prior to the cremation there will be shadow puppet performances or displays of the *barong landong* dance.

The actual burning usually takes around three hours, during which time the family goes home to rest. When they return to the cremation ground in the late afternoon it is for a more private, small-scale ceremony. The ashes have now been gathered and placed in a yellow coconut. They are taken in procession to a local river, or to the sea, and are there scattered on the water after another brief ritual.

ABOVE: "Suddenly the body emerges. It's wrapped in white at the end of the sheet, and it's quickly bundled into the tower" (see p. 49).
BELOW: cremation bulls.

MAGIC AND WITCHCRAFT

The Balinese won't talk about it much but they all believe in witches. Certain people become witches *(leyak)* by undergoing a series of rituals, reciting mantras backwards and the like, and the disembodied spirits of these people can be seen as green lights hovering in graveyards or at crossroads, or as animals encountered in the dark.

Though these beliefs certainly have their origins in the pre-Hindu past, they nevertheless are embraced by the Hindu world view. Negative forces are simply the opposites of the positive ones used by the temple priests. Each is a part of existence, and security is best safeguarded by ensuring a balance between the two natural sets of forces. It's the left and right of the shadow puppet plays in another form.

Most Balinese drama originates in temple ceremony (just as Western drama originated in religious performances in ancient Greece), and these dramas often involve possession, or are staged as exorcism rituals. What appears to the Western observer as "culture" is actually spiritual, not only in its origin but in present-day significance to the participants.

Whether it's a performance of the *barong* dance, the provision by a *balian* (herbalist/witch doctor/faith healer) of an amulet against illness, or the rituals surrounding *kanda empat* (see BIRTH, CHILDHOOD, LOVE AND MARRIAGE, p. 32), life in Bali proceeds according to very different tenets than those the writers of the tourist brochures would like to have you believe.

The Barong Dance at Batubulan (see p.68). This good-natured monster overcomes the powerful *rangda* in ritual conflict, with a little bit of help from his friends. This popular dance is really an exorcism ritual aimed at limiting the power of the *rangda*, a kind of witch.

HEROES AND VILLAINS

Ideally, anyone hoping to come to grips with Balinese culture on a serious level ought to read something of the great Indian romance, the *Ramayana*, beforehand. This is rather like saying a visitor to England should read *A Christmas Carol* or *Hamlet*, and whereas this too would undoubtedly be a good idea, it's unlikely many visitors, even those with cultural aspirations, will actually take the trouble.

Nevertheless, the ancient Sanskrit poems, the *Ramayana* and the *Mahabharata*, do still have a very pervasive influence on the Balinese, even though not one in ten thousand will have read a single line of them. Reading isn't the main means of cultural transmission in Asia, and even the epics themselves were passed on for millennia by recitation before they were ever written down. And in Bali today it is through the shadow puppet plays and the dance dramas that the people make contact with these ancient symbolic stories. It's comparable to the Middle Ages in Europe where few read the scriptures but everyone followed the religion and knew the stories of Adam and Eve, Abraham and Isaac, David and Goliath, Noah's Ark, and the birth and death of Jesus through church festivals, street dramas, paintings and stained-glass windows.

As the average visitor is only in Bali for a short time, and the shadow plays (for instance) will be in several incomprehensible languages, it will perhaps be useful to give a very brief description of these two great works, and the crucial episodes returned to time and time again by Balinese dancers and shadow puppeteers.

The *Ramayana* (*The Romance of Rama*) is an immensely long poem, 48,000 lines, completed probably around 300 BC by one Valmiki, a sage who himself appears as a character in the poem.

Prince Rama, the perfect ruler and an incarnation of Vishnu (Wisnu in Bali) wins Sita to be his wife by bending the bow of the god Shiva (Siwa in Bali) at a tournament. Rama is heir to the throne of the kingdom of Ayodhya but is disinherited and forced into exile in the forest with his wife and his half-brother Laksmana.

One day, while Rama and Laksmana are pursuing a golden deer, the demon king Ravana (who has sent the deer specifically to distract Rama) seizes Sita and carries her off to his island kingdom of Lanka.

But Rama is helped by the forest monkeys, by their king Sugriva and especially by their warrior-general, the white monkey Hanuman. It's he who discovers where Sita is and leads Rama to her. In the inevitable battle that follows, Rama wins back Sita, and also, by and by, his own throne.

But the people suspect poor Sita of infidelity to Rama while she was on Lanka, and Rama is forced to place her in a hermitage. There she gives birth to Rama's twin sons and meets the sage Valmiki.

Eventually, when her sons are grown up, Sita is accepted back by the people and by Rama, but, weary of life, asks the earth to take her, which it duly does.

Already, from this brief outline, many Balinese echoes are apparent. There's a *losmen* called Ayodhya at Lovina, there's a statue of Hanuman at the entrance to the Monkey Forest at Sangeh, and the story of Rama and the deer is at the heart of the Ramayana Ballet dance.

If the *Ramayana* is long, the *Mahabharata* is positively sprawling. It's three times the length of the Old and New Testaments of the Bible put together, 200,000 lines of Sanskrit verse. And, like the Bible, it is in fact a storehouse of the history, laws, poetry and moral principles of an entire people. It was probably only revised by its supposed author, one Vyasa,

OPPOSITE: the figure of an official in the Barong Dance. The courts of the old Hindu rajahs of Java and Bali have left their mark on a number of Balinese dramas.

any time between 400 BC and AD 400. Its title means *The Great Epic of the Bharata Dynasty*, and it's the longest poem known anywhere in the world.

The main channel in this vast and complex river of words is the story of the feud between the rival branches of a royal family, the Pandavas and the Kauravas.

Who should rule has been rendered unclear by the eldest son of the previous generation being passed over for the

succession because he's blind, and then the next in line giving up the throne to become an ascetic and the blind son being brought back to rule. On his death, his five sons are forced to flee the court and go into exile, together with the wife they all share, Draupadi. They are joined by their cousin Krishna. Eventually they return, but are forced to flee a second time when the eldest brother loses everything in a dice game with his cousin.

War becomes inescapable, and battle rages for 18 days on the field of Kuruksetra, north of modern-day Delhi. Only seven individuals survive the immense conflict, among them the five brothers and Krishna.

Krishna is later shot, mistaken for a deer, and the five brothers set out to seek the heaven of Indra in the company of a dog, really the god Dharma in disguise. Only the eldest, Yudhisthira, eventually completes the quest.

Part of Book Six of the *Mahabharata* is the celebrated "Bhagavadgita" ("Song of the Lord"). It's a dialogue between Arjuna, one of the Pandava brothers, and Krishna before the battle. Anticipating the terrible destruction that is certain to take place, Arjuna asks if it is really right that he should fight to kill his own kith and kin in this way. Krishna replies with the doctrine of the disinterested discharge of one's duty, and in the process reveals himself as a reincarnation of the god Vishnu.

But the "Bhagavadgita," far from endorsing a militaristic ethic, goes on to encompass the heart of Hindu belief as to the nature of God, and the means of approach for the awakened soul to this supreme reality.

What is notable about the poem as a whole is the way it manifests the values of a warrior society, and then proceeds to add to these religious values that finally supersede the heroic ones and even point the way forward to the later Indian principles of non-violence and philosophical pacifism.

The stories contained in these two poems spread alongside Indian religion east into Cambodia and south to what is now Indonesia. That incidents from these epics are still so alive, and so popular, not only in India itself (where they form the material for the *kathakali* dance dramas) but as far south as Java and Bali is surely one of the lesser, but nonetheless most remarkable, wonders of the world.

Balinese dancers. Their costumes are made and maintained with an extraordinary care and attention to detail.

THE BALINESE AT PLAY

SILVER RAIN

Old Balinese princes used to pay for the formation of large and splendid orchestras *(gamelan)* in which they then performed themselves, no doubt with considerable display of self-congratulation, rather as the princelings of eighteenth-century German courts would play the cello or the flute and elicit works with prominent, but not too difficult, parts for their instrument from Bach or Mozart.

This patronage by the jovial rajahs of old, dividing their time between *gamelan*-playing and the demands of their innumerable wives, has given way to support by the local community associations *(banjar)* and a competitive ambiance fostered by the training courses in *gamelan* music given by the colleges of higher education in Denpasar.

Though the *gamelan* derive historically from the indigenous orchestras of old Java, the music they play in Bali today is altogether more lively and progressive than anything you'll hear on the larger island. Though it may seem at first that what you're hearing is a highly stylized and traditional art form, the truth is that new styles within that form are constantly being evolved, and Balinese *gamelan* music is very much a living and growing genre.

What characterizes the Balinese *gamelan* is its brilliance of sound, its sudden changes of volume and pace, and its virtuoso displays of very precise, very fast playing.

Two key features have to be understood. As with Balinese drama, the performers are not professional, and the music exists primarily as an accompaniment to rituals and dance performances (themselves also accompaniments to rituals) rather than as an entertainment in its own right. Of course, there are exceptions nowadays, such as the uprooted and rather sad-looking performers seated in the lobbies of some big hotels playing with commendable spirit for a set portion of every hour. But the overwhelming majority of the musicians in Bali are farmers during the day, and very highly trained *gamelan* artists after sundown.

If you want to judge how genuine the *gamelan* you're seeing is, count the number of performers. A real *gamelan gong*, the commonest type of modern band, will

have around twenty players and feature the following instruments:

– xylophone-like instruments known as *gangsa*. These consist of bronze keys over bamboo resonators that are beaten with a mallet held in the right hand and their reverberation immediately cut short by the thumb and index finger of the left.

– a *riong*, a frame holding bronze "pots" which four players strike with sticks.

– a *trompong*, an instrument similar to the above but played by a virtuoso solo player.

– a *ceng ceng*, a frame with many cymbals suspended from it – these are struck by another, hand-held cymbal.

– *kendang*, drums. These are the heart of the *gamelan*, the only instruments the

Balinese *gamelan* musicians. The music is almost entirely percussive in nature and has been described by one writer as "a shining rain of silver", by another as "the muffled laughter of forgotten gods".

dancers need attend to and played by the seasoned maestros of the orchestra. The first drummer is like the first violinist and conductor of a Western classical orchestra combined, the leader and controller of the *gamelan*.

The musicians will all be male, will be seated on the ground and dressed in the brilliant uniform of their particular orchestra.

The instruments are of invariable pitch, fixed forever at the time of manufacture. Where instruments are paired, there is often a slight and deliberate difference between their respective pitches designed to set up a deliciously thrilling dissonance that is an essential component in the brilliant, metallic cascade of sound that is Balinese music.

Here, then, is a music that, unless extra instruments are added, is entirely percussive. Nothing could be further removed from the Western classical tradition where the timpani have the lowest status of all the instruments in the orchestra. In Bali, they are everything, and the result is a music that injects energy into the sultry night air, a music so vibrant and electrifying that the name *kebyar gamelan* says it all. *Kebyar* means bursting into flower, flaring up suddenly into jagged, passionate brilliance.

The American Colin McPhee, author of *A House in Bali* (see BIBLIOGRAPHY) can be credited with first bringing this unique music to the notice of the West. He must have known his own attempts to transcribe the music for two pianos were doomed from the start, but the influence persisted nonetheless, in America especially, and found its first major flowering on the international scene in the sixties with the music of such artists as Steve Reich, Terry Riley and, later, Philip Glass.

Gamelan music and street processions often combine to add delight to the most oppressively humid day.

THE BALINESE AT PLAY

DANCE AND DRAMA

While only men play in the *gamelan* orchestras, the dance dramas are truly androgynous, with women and men dancing a wide variety of roles, sometimes as the opposite sex, sometimes as their own, and sometimes as animals. The style is essentially Javanese, and before that Indian, but with Balinese spirit-ritual elements added.

Training is very intensive and begins young. Balinese dance has always made great use of children, and girls destined for the *legong* dance start at six or seven with training that includes special massage to make their limbs supple. Hand and head movements are especially important, leg movements – in total contrast to Western dance of all styles – less so. Facial expressions and the movement of the eyes are most important of all.

Despite the long training, dancers are not paid, at least not when performing traditional festival dances at the temples. The wide variety of dances in Bali is always being added to, old styles falling out of favor and new ones coming into fashion. In this, Balinese dance contrasts with the unaltering classical dance of Java from which it derives. The difference comes from dance in Bali being a popular art form, rooted in collective social organizations, whereas in Java it was for centuries something performed under the patronage of the rajahs and nowadays is staged almost exclusively for tourists.

Balinese dances were originally, and are still generally, sacred, performed to greet the gods as they descend from their mountain-top homes into the temples to attend the temple ceremonies.

However, special abbreviated dance shows are now put on specifically for visitors. These take place either at the bigger hotels at Sanur or Nusa Dua or in villages such as Ubud, Batubulan or Bona.

There won't be any Balinese at these tourist shows, apart from the odd child selling soft drinks or "programs" who might stay on to watch. There will be raked seating provided so that everyone gets an uninterrupted view, there will be an attempt at modern theatrical lighting, and the shows will begin at a convenient time.

But what you will see will not be the dance drama, performed in the crowded forecourt of a temple attended by the entire village population dressed for a high festival, that made Bali famous in the thirties. Not only will any performance done as a routine for an audience the artists know have little if any knowledge of the art form inevitably lack fire; the whole context will be missing, and what you will be witnessing will be an art torn up from its roots and presented in a vacuum.

Nevertheless, there are of course different levels of artistry in these shows, and it should be said at once that the dances at **Ubud**, the large village north of Denpasar that is the "cultural capital" of Bali, are usually of a high quality and only the original social context is missing.

At Ubud, a different program is offered each night of the week, either at the Ubud Palace or elsewhere. Where the performances are outside the village itself, transport is provided and the cost included in the price of the ticket.

The *legong* performance, currently presented on Mondays at the Palace, is really a kind of revue. It features a number of different dances, with the *legong* itself some two-thirds of the way through. The standard is very high and, despite the fact that this performance is put on exclusively for the benefit of foreigners, this is an excellent introduction to Balinese dance.

Danced against a background of the temple, the combination of the hard, precise music, the rich costumes, and the

---

All the sultry, languid beauty of the tropics is suggested by this young performer in the Barong Dance. Children are trained in the art of dance from an early age, and then often continue to perform throughout their adukt lives.

dedication on the faces of the young performers are very powerful. That the lighting is improvised, some of it consisting of domestic lightbulbs with biscuit-tin reflectors, only adds to the authenticity and excitement of the performance.

At **Bona**, half an hour's drive east of Denpasar, shows are given nightly at various sites. The village is not easily accessible by public transport after sunset and audiences are almost invariably brought in by the various tour agencies in Kuta and Sanur. The performance areas, lit by torches in preparation for the *kecak* dance, make a picturesque sight as you drive past them in the early Indonesian dark. The performances themselves, however, can be rather less impressive.

The standard fare at Bona is a *kecak* dance followed by two spirit possession dances, the *sanghyang dedari* and the *sanghyang jaran*. The convenience of this arrangement for the organizers is that none of these dances requires a *gamelan* accompaniment.

At **Batubulan**, north of Denpasar on the road to Gianyar, *barong* dances are performed, again exclusively for visitors, at 9 am every morning. The show lasts an hour.

Bali's Dances

The following are the main dances and other dramatic performances you are likely to encounter on the island.

Arja   Sometimes referred to as "Balinese opera," this is really ballet and opera combined. Four women, playing male characters, sing and dance simultaneously. Clowns and servants provide the low-life commentary.

Baris Gede   A warrior dance for a group of a dozen or so middle-aged men, its purpose is to protect the visiting gods at

A gorgeously clad figure from the Kecak Dance approaches the flaming lamp that is this dance's only illumination. The dance has no instrumental accompaniment and is based on a story from the Indian *Ramayana* epic.

temple festivals from evil spirits. The dancers wear headdresses with a triangle of white cloth at the back, and with pieces of shell attached. They carry spears tipped with peacock feathers, and during the dance divide into two groups and engage in mock conflict.

Baris Pendet   A solo form of the above. In this demanding virtuoso dance, the performer goes through all the emotions of a warrior before, and then in, battle.

Barong   Essentially an exorcism dance, the *barong* features a benign monster – the *barong ket* – rather like the lion in the Chinese lion dance, but with long white hair and fitted with leather saddles. Its mouth opens and shuts noisily. Its opponent is the *rangda*, a witch with long white hair, drooping breasts, bulging eyes and twisted fangs, and flourishing a magically powerful white cloth.

The full version begins with introductory dances unconnected to the main action – a comic confrontation between the *barong* and three masked palm-wine tappers, and a short *legong* dance.

The play proper's essential feature is a battle between the good-natured *barong* and the *rangda*, with the *barong* assisted, not very effectively, by a group of men armed with *keris* (short swords). What leads up to this is a plot involving a queen who has to sacrifice her son to the goddess of death. The son is saved, being given immortality by the god Siwa, but takes on a variety of heroic tasks which quickly prove too much for him. He calls on the *barong* for help, and the *barong* in turn calls on the armed warriors.

The *rangda* puts a spell on the men so that they try to kill themselves. The *barong*, however, renders their swords harmless, and the impotent frenzy of the entranced warriors is a big feature of the show.

In the sword (*kris*) dance, usually seen as the culmination of a temple's *odalan* festival, entranced men attempt to wound themselves with sharpened weapons. They never succeed.

THE BALINESE AT PLAY

The *rangda* is finally defeated, but real magic is considered to have been brought forth by the performance – and indeed the warriors are often in an actual trance by this stage – and so a chicken is sacrificed and water sprinkled on the warriors by a resident *pemangku* as a conclusion to the dance.

Barong Landong   The name means "tall barong," and this performance features two large figures, twice life size, manipulated by actors inside them. They enact a comic slanging-match between a black giant, *jero gede*, and his woman, *jero luh*. The little chanted drama is accompanied by a few musicians and is in reality a rite to dispel evil performed on important occasions such as the night before a cremation.

Calon Arang   An exorcism drama aimed at the local village witches (*leyak* – see MAGIC AND WITCHCRAFT, p. 54) and performed when a new temple is dedicated.

Staged at the full moon, and continuing until dawn, the drama features the witch *rangda* who, at the climax of the performance, after comic interludes and dances by young girls, emerges from her house and advances in a frenzy on the audience.

The part of the *rangda* is taken by an experienced older actor because the performance involves the witch going into an entranced rage, possessed – so the Balinese believe – by the spirit of the actual *rangda*. The end of the event is unpredictable, and the *rangda* can on occasion run amok. Only an actor of long experience can hope to control so powerful a spirit entering into him.

The purpose of the performance is to placate the *rangda* by demonstrating her power, and thus gain her cooperation against the lesser witches in the village.

The performance raises many profound questions, such as the extent to which any acting anywhere is a form of self-imposed possession, and the reasons for the worldwide obsession with solitary women past the age of childbearing as agents of evil (*rangda* means widow).

Gambuh   An ancient Balinese dance performed to entertain visiting gods at temple festivals. Speaking in Kawi, a prince and his beloved undergo various trials to the accompaniment of an antique orchestra featuring bass flutes. Comic servants provide a commentary in Low Balinese.

Janger   Twelve girls and 12 boys sit on four sides of a square with a leader in the middle. They perform a variety of dances, comic sketches and acrobatic displays.

Jauk   A short dance by a masked dancer displaying the sinister convolutions of a demon.

Joged   A non-temple dance that was much appreciated by early visitors to the island anxious to penetrate the ceremonious reserve of the Balinese. A solo girl dances flirtatiously with men she selects from the audience. Sometimes it is performed by a boy dressed as a woman, in which case it's called *gandrung*.

OPPOSITE: the sword (*kris*) dance demonstrated at a show for tourists; ABOVE: the evil *rangda* from the Barong Dance. Dance is arguably the finest flower of Balinese art.

Kebiyar Duduk   The Balinese emphasis on eyes, head and arms in dance, as opposed to legs, is highlighted in this dance for a solo seated performer. It's essentially an abstract interpretation of Balinese music and was invented in the thirties by the famous Balinese dancer known as Mario – his career is described by Covarrubias in *The Island of Bali* (see BIBLIOGRAPHY).

Kecak   There is no accompanying orchestra in this dance. Instead, a large group of men provides a continuous vocal background, something like a sound-picture of an ocean in all its moods. They are dressed only in a black and white check sarong, with a red flower behind the right ear and a white one behind the left.

They move around on their haunches, sometimes swaying from this side to that, sometimes bouncing up and down, sometimes flinging themselves forward in a circle with arms outstretched toward the center. All the time they utter a non-verbal chant, sometimes in unison, sometimes contrapuntally between sections of the group.

The central performance area is lit only by a flaming lamp, but the gorgeously clad characters in the drama to which the group of men provide an accompaniment usually arrive on the scene through a temple gateway, dramatically lit from behind.

The story is of Rama's trip to the forest with Sita to seek the golden deer. Rawana, king of the demons, kidnaps Sita, but Hanuman, the white monkey, comes to her aid by telling Rama what's happened. A son of the demon king fires an arrow (that turns into a snake) at Rama, but Rama calls on Garuda, the bird god, to save him. The king of the monkeys, Sugriwa, then arrives on the scene and the drama ends with a fight between the monkeys and the demons, with the *kecak* chorus dividing in support of the two sides. Rama is reunited with his beloved Sita.

Kupu Kupu Carum   A dance in which a prince manages through meditation to overcome the temptations offered him by a band of nymphs. The actor playing the prince remains motionless throughout most of the performance.

Legong   This most classical of all Balinese dances used only to be performed by girls who had not yet reached puberty. It is performed by three dancers, two of them enacting the principal characters and the third playing the *condong* or servant.

The dance is so formalized, with the dancers portraying first one incident then another without any change of style, that it is very difficult to follow what's going on. But, for the record, the plot involves a princess, Rangkesari, who has been forcibly abducted by a prince, Lasem. She refuses to have anything to do with him, and when she hears her brother, the crown prince of Kahuripan, is coming to save her, she appeals to her captor to release her and so avoid a battle. He refuses, and on his way out to fight sees a raven, an omen of his imminent defeat on the battlefield.

The dance tells only a fragment of this brief story. It begins with the *condong* dancing a prologue, then shows the two identically dressed girls as the prince and princess. The prince is already about to leave for the battlefield when they first appear. He is sad that the princess has rejected him; she asks him not to fight her brother; he refuses and leaves. The *condong* then closes the performance by appearing with little gilt wings attached, representing the bird of ill omen.

Such highly stylized dramatic forms, showing only the climax of a story already well known to the audience, and even that symbolically and without any actual confrontation, has characterized highly developed forms of theater elsewhere, in ancient Greece and in Japan, for example. Here in Bali, the *legong* has a particularly

---

A young girl dancer at a performance at Bona. The usual offering here is a Kecak, a Sanghyang Dedari ("Virgin Dance") and a Sanghyang Jaran ("Fire Dance").

remote quality given to it by its being played by (originally) very young girls dressed in exceptionally elaborate costumes.

There is no mention of the *legong* in the ancient *lontar* (palm-leaf books) referring to dance, and the form was probably created as recently as the nineteenth century.

Mendet (also known as *Pendet*) A dance to welcome the spirits to the temple performed by a group of older women carrying offerings in their right hands.

Oleg Tambulilingan A dance representing the flirtation between two bees gathering honey among the flowers.

Panyembrama A welcoming dance performed by a troupe of girls who scatter flowers on the spectators. It was evolved in the sixties as an introductory dance for the "*legong* revue" performances.

Prembon A masked dance showing the defeat by Sri Krisna Kapakisan of rebellious subjects using a magical sword given him by Gaja Mada.

Ramayana Ballet Imported to Bali recently from Java, this dance tells the story of Rama and Hanuman (the white monkey) from the *Ramayana* epic. It's the same story told in the *kecak* dance.

Rejang A stately, processional movement performed by women bringing offerings to a temple.

Sanghyang Dedari (also called the Virgin Dance) A possession dance in which two young girl dancers are put into a trance. The only music is chanting by unaccompanied voices.

Sanghyang Jaran (also called the Fire Dance) An event rather than a dance in which a young man enters riding a hobbyhorse and proceeds to trample with his bare feet on a pile of smoldering coconut husks. The performer is in a trance and sometimes kicks the glowing shells around quite violently. They're raked back into a heap by an assistant. Afterwards, the entranced youth is brought back to normal consciousness with water. He then drinks holy water three times and offers blossoms three times in the direction of the temple.

Topeng Pajegan A masked dance in which a solo dancer performs in a series of different masks to portray a variety of characters in a story.

Topeng Panca A masked dance in which a number of dancers, each wearing a different mask, act out a story.

Topeng Tua A solo masked dance, slow and deliberate, in which the dancer imitates the uncertain and painful movements of a very old man.

Wayang Wong A rare form of drama where actors enact the stories from the shadow puppet plays.

You can attend dance classes, held in the mornings, at two colleges in the capital – see DENPASAR section for details.

A six-week Bali Arts Festival is held in Denpasar from mid-June to the end of July every year featuring a good deal of music and dance.

Finally, the Badung Government Tourist Office on Jalan Surapati in Denpasar (© 23399 and 23602) issues an up-to-date broadsheet with details of imminent temple festivals, many of which will include dance performances.

ABOVE: Kecak Dance; OPPOSITE: seated dancer – arms and eyes are far more important in Balinese dance than the legs, and this makes it far removed from every kind of Western dance. It is, of course, Indian in origin.

SHADOWS IN THE DARK

The shadow-puppet play (*wayang* – puppet, *kulit* – leather) you are most likely to see will have been staged specifically for tourists. But there are at least a couple of dozen practicing puppeteers in Bali staging performances on request for weddings, temple anniversaries and the night before cremations.

The *wayang kulit* is, like almost all art in Bali, ceremonial in origin, and the puppeteer *(dalang)* a kind of magician.

The artist as seer is an old idea, and it's no surprise that the Indonesian puppet play – it's also found in Java – is seen by many as a form of metaphysics. Sukarno, the country's first president, used to gather his ministers together in his hill-station retreat and tease them with puppet shows which they didn't have to look very far to see prefigured their advancement or fall from grace. Even now there are commentators who attribute the blank passivity of the people in the face of the massacre of leftists in 1965 to a fatalism rooted in the mythology of the *wayang*, a belief that, in the eternal battle between good and evil, there was no hope for you if, in the episode of the drama which happened to constitute your life, you were unfortunate enough to be caught on the wrong side of the stage.

The "stage" in the *wayang* is a cloth screen some one meter by three. The right as you, the audience, view it is the side of the bug-eyed villains, the left of the strangely emaciated aristocratic heroes.

On a low platform behind the screen sits the *dalang*, cross-legged and formally dressed as if for a religious ceremony, which in a way this is. To his left is the puppet box containing a large selection of the puppets in regular use. Behind him, dressed in sarong and headdress, sit the musicians of the *gender wayang* behind their *gangsa*, the xylophone-like instruments of the *gamelan*. No gongs or drums are used, and the *gangsa* are struck by hammers held in each hand. Consequently the reverberation has to be stopped by the knuckles rather than the left hand as in the *gamelan* proper.

The performance begins with an overture by the musicians during which the puppeteer sprinkles holy water and makes offerings to sanctify the show and "bring the puppets to life." The show itself begins with a kind of skeletal leaf (but actually the sacred Tree of Life) dividing the screen. It will be used again later to indicate changes of scene.

The stories are all taken from the *Ramayana* and *Mahabharata* epics (see HEROES AND VILLAINS, p. 57) and are well known in advance to the Balinese, just as the story of Cinderella will be known in advance to Western audiences at a pantomime, or *Don Giovanni* to the operagoer. The attraction of the performance is both the telling-over of an old tale and the up-to-date and local references the *dalang* will manage somehow or other to incorporate into it.

It's as well the stories are known already because the actual narration will be chanted in the dead Javanese language of Kawi, and the language of the ordinary people will only appear in the sarcastic and debunking remarks of the four low-life "clowns".

Thus at every *wayang* play not only does society witness a highlighting and a confirmation of the established social order, it also is made conscious of the interplay of this world with that of the gods, and in a way that makes life seem just a part of a greater enactment over which it's foolish to think we have any measure of control.

It's important to realize you have every right to go backstage and watch the show from the other side. There'll even be a couple of benches provided, one on each

The *wayang kulit*, or shadow-puppet play. The *dalang*, or puppeteer, sits behind his screen and selects his puppets from a collection in a large wooden box. The stories are well-known to the local audience in advance – they have to be as only the jokes are in a language the ordinary people understand.

side of the performers. And it's here, behind the scenes, that the real atmosphere of the *wayang* can best be flavored.

It's an enclosed, primordial scene. The flaming lamp, clearly visible even from front-of-house and giving the flickering effect of early film to the show as a whole, is seen backstage as being a giant kettle with flames leaping from its stubby, wick-crammed spout.

The puppets themselves, you'll see, are intricately shaped, and painted in great

detail, with much gilt – quite unnecessarily for their function as casters of shadows, but very appropriately for sacral adjuncts. A string, worked by the *dalang*'s index finger, moves the puppet's jaw, while a thin stick, manipulated with the puppeteer's other hand, operates the arm of any character that appears solo.

An assistant sits on either side of the puppeteer and prepares and then hands

The *wayang kulit*. ABOVE: the puppeteer, both magician and priest, both jester and guardian of an extraordinarily ancient tradition. OPPOSITE: the primordial scene backstage – you're welcome to go round and take a look. On the whole it's more exciting that out front.

him the puppets as he needs them from a banana tree trunk into which they've been stuck ready for use. The puppets' traveling box stands away to the puppeteer's left and, sitting cross-legged, he beats on the box with a peg held between the toes of his right foot, providing rhythmic excitement and special effects for the innumerable fights into which the stories always and rather quickly descend.

The puppeteer does all the talking, telling the story and acting all the speaking parts. Sweat running down his face from the hot night and the heat of the lamp, he pours out a stream of jokes, chants and heroic invocations, beating the screen with his flimsy puppets and simultaneously hammering the box with his foot.

The guttering flame is replenished by the "evil-side" (puppeteer's left) attendant pouring oil into the lidless kettle. A shield behind concentrates the light onto the screen and keeps it out of the eyes of the puppeteer. The costumed musicians hammer away, interweaving their arpeggios and changing rhythm for every new scene and facet of the immemorially ancient story.

It's an extraordinary scene, these stories from far-off India being reenacted in the tropical night and with such a combination of relish and formality. The eager, laughing faces of the audience, the constant reversing of the puppets, so that they appear first facing this way and then that, and each change accompanied by a clack with the toe-hammer. The old tackle, the flaring light, the relish of the exuberant puppeteer... it's akin to the Sicilian puppets of Palermo re-enacting stories of the crusades based on the rhyming epics of Ariosto or Tasso. It has the same enclosed quality, the same intensity.

Here in the tropics it's older still. What you're seeing is something so old that scholars are unable to ascribe a place of origin to it. Yet here it is being re-created yet again in this wall-less village hall, by the sweating, laughing but be-hatted puppeteer.

It's the magic of the old Javanese night. And the puppeteer, as well as actually being a priest, is also a magician, able to bring to life these ancient stories with his two-dimensional dolls. He stirs the naturally symbolic imaginations of the people, warming their easily warmed hearts with his gusto and his mixture of heroism and broad popular comedy.

The popularity of these old night entertainments shows how deep they go into the

THE AFFRIGHTED SUN

The gamecock clipped and armed for fight
Does the rising sun affright.

William Blake, *Auguries of Innocence (1805)*

The tending and care of fighting cocks is one of the most visible parts of Balinese life, and men sitting in circles preening their birds is one of the commonest sights on the island.

consciousness of the people. These flickering images in jungle villages beside elaborately wrought Hindu temples have for centuries molded the souls of a naturally artistic people with stories of magic, power struggles, good and evil, and seemingly pointless heroism.

When in 1909 the Balinese aristocracy presented themselves before the Dutch army for certain destruction in long lines of bejeweled and costumed splendor, the images and patterns of the heroic tales of the *wayang kulit* cannot have been far from their hearts. Like the Pandavas and the Kouravas at war in the *Mahabharata*, they could never surrender.

All gambling has been illegal throughout Indonesia since 1981. In Bali, however, where the letting of blood is deemed a necessary part of temple festivals, permits are issued by the police allowing three cockfights on the days of temple anniversary celebrations. Both the restriction on the number of fights and the general prohibition on gambling are regularly ignored on these occasions.

Bets are placed nominally in the ancient currency of the ringgit though in reality in the rupiah equivalent. A lay priest (*pemangku*) gives offerings to both the good and evil spirits before the fight begins.

The Balinese for cockfights is *tajen* (blades), the razor-sharp knives that are attached to the cocks' left legs.

Cocks naturally fight each other over the female birds, and this is what they do in the trial bouts you can see on any sunny afternoon. But it's only with these lethal blades attached that they slash their opponent almost to death, often in a matter of seconds. They don't experience the blades in the trial bouts, of course. Then suddenly, in the fight itself, nature

becomes hideously armed, and a flurry in the air becomes a flashing of steel, with the defeated bird lying bleeding in the dust.

This isn't the end. The blade becomes the property of the specialist *(pekembar)* the owner has employed to fix it in place. As soon as the winner has been declared, the legs, the blade attached, are chopped

off the losing cock, almost invariably while it is still alive.

To deplore this casual cruelty may be judged a Western prejudice inappropriate to Asia, but the pain is real enough for the cock wherever it happens. I have seen Balinese cocks lying exhausted and wounded, suffering the humiliation of defeat and the agony of laceration, start up from the earth at what is clearly the most horrific pain imaginable. And this is the eventual fate reserved for every one of the creatures so lovingly caressed by their doting owners of former days.

CRICKET-FIGHTING

The Balinese also bet on crickets; it's a sort of poor-man's cockfighting. The creatures are caught in the cracks of the dried-out rice fields after harvest and fed on grains of rice and flower petals. They are exercised and bathed, and kept in tubular cages made of sections of bamboo. The fights take place inside a pair of cages placed together end to end. The winner is the cricket that forces the other to retreat to its furthest corner. Bets are in the region of a few thousand rupiah – on cocks they can be millions.

BIRD ORCHESTRAS

Bells and small flutes are attached round the necks of doves so that when they wheel overhead they produce a delicious tinkling and humming. Covarrubias says in *The Island of Bali* (see BIBLIOGRAPHY) that these aerial musical instruments are a protection against birds of prey. And it is true that if this is not the case, then bird orchestras are the only form of Balinese music created purely for pleasure.

Even so, it would be very Balinese to make them for fun, and then say they were to accompany the gods on their way down to the temples. Whatever their original purpose, the unexpected sound of these tiny instruments borne on the breeze is one of the real delights of the island.

ABOVE: a fighting cock and its master; OPPOSITE: men preening and matching their fighting cocks – a common sight all over Bali. Cock fights are nowadays only permitted before temple anniversary ceremonies as a precaution against excessive gambling.

THE BALINESE AT PLAY

ARTS AND CRAFTS

PAINTING

Some people go to Bali to buy paintings. Balinese art acquired some celebrity before the war due to the publicity given it by artists from the West coming to live on the island. They found a prolific but static local tradition, and encouraged the practitioners to experiment on semi-

remains there is a vast amount of junk being produced merely to satisfy the most elementary preconceptions as to what a painting by a Balinese artist might be like.

Much of the worst can be bypassed by going direct to Ubud, the center for Balinese painting both good and mediocre. Here at least you will have a chance to inspect a wide range of work – particularly conveniently at the gallery set apart across a rice field to the left of the Puri Lukisan Museum where paintings by

Western lines. The results proved exotic yet familiar, just the thing the well-heeled tourists of the period needed to take home as mementos. But the truth is, things aren't what they were.

It may well be true that you can resell Balinese pictures in the Gulf States and elsewhere for a handsome profit, if you know where to take them. But the fact

many artists hang with prices (not necessarily final) attached. A visit here will allow you to compare styles and going rates before you begin looking at the galleries showing only the owner's work.

Balinese painting before the thirties was exclusively concerned with the production of hangings and calendars for temples. Production was centered on Kamasan, south of Klungkung, and work of this kind is now referred to as being in the Kamasan style. Subjects were scenes from the epic stories, painted in hand-ground paints, and the final result was not unlike a colored version of the *wayang kulit* shadow puppet plays. These kind of

ABOVE and OPPOSITE: the terrors that await evil-doers in the afterlife, and the glee with which their tormentors go about their work, are vividly depicted on the walls of the Kertha Gosa (the ancient Court House) in Klungkung. The pictures are modern copies of older originals.

paintings are still available, and still being produced, in Kamasan itself.

For the rest, styles are nowadays divided into "traditional" and "young artists." By traditional is meant the style of painting encouraged in the thirties by the Western artists Rudolf Bonnet and Walter Spies, painters who settled in Bali and lived in Campuhan, down by Ubud's suspension bridge. These pictures depict daily scenes as well as legendary ones, in restrained colors or even monochrome. They are comparatively realistic, though filling every corner of the canvas with detail, and lacking any real attempt at light and shade effects.

The so-called young artists were set to work by the Dutch painter Arie Smit in the sixties and are based in Penestanan, an extension of Ubud just over the bridge from Campuhan. Their pictures are vividly colored naive versions of daily-life scenes.

Of course there are some fine pictures among all these, though originality is not a strong suit in the Balinese hand. But prices are not low, whatever the quality – you will have to start thinking in terms of at least US$200 as your absolute minimum if you want to acquire anything at all reasonable, and that would be for a small-sized production.

The craftsmen of earlier times were occupied with carving figures of gods and heroes for the adornment of the palaces of the local rajahs. The depiction of animals and trees, as well as non-traditional fantasy figures, came with the arrival of Western artists. A particular style involving smooth surfaces and elongated human bodies has become common, and is often looked on as quintessentially Balinese, but actually is only something evolved in the thirties in imitation of the European Art Nouveau style.

As with all art objects, the only advice that can be given is to buy only what you yourself consider to be of high quality. Despite the endless duplication, there are some wonderful craftsmen at work. Fashioning the wood with delicate steel tools and a lightweight hammer, and working with extraordinary speed, they have gained the reputation of being among of the finest wood-carvers anywhere in the world.

Painted carvings, made from local soft woods, are cheap and produced in huge numbers. Imitation fruit – bananas in particular – are almost all produced in the village of Pujung (see THE BROAD HIGHWAY, p. 102), yet can be found on sale all over the world.

Hardwood carvings are generally produced using imported wood as Bali's climate does not give rise to classic equatorial rain forests. Ebony, for instance, is imported from Kalimantan and Sulawesi in eastern Indonesia.

Beware of imitations of these woods. If you want to be sure your ebony is ebony, there's one sure-fire test: ebony doesn't float. Whether your retailer will allow you to test it is, of course, another matter.

The famous shop for wood-carvings in Mas is Ida Bagus Tilem's. This is where presidents and millionaires buy their Bali souvenirs. Quality is guaranteed, but

The booklet *Different Styles of Painting in Bali* by Drs Sudarmaji, available at the Neka Gallery in Ubud (not to be confused with the Museum Neka) is helpful in the early stages in getting an idea of what to expect.

WOOD-CARVING

Balinese wood-carving is renowned because a natural local aptitude has allowed itself to be influenced by sophisticated Western styles, and the resulting hybrid artifacts consequently differ from anything found anywhere else. The main place to see wood-carvings in Bali is the village of Mas, south of Ubud.

A Balinese painting from a private collection. The rural scene, and the crowding of the canvas with largely decorative detail, is very typical of the so-called "traditional" school of painting.

prices are very high: a place, perhaps, to see the best, then seek out comparable specimens in the numerous smaller establishments elsewhere in the village.

THE OTHER FACE

Masks are an important element in Balinese dance, and foreigners have been quick to see them as eminently desirable items.

Every actor knows the power of a mask. Hanging on a wall, it's just decorative. Put it on and, in an extraordinary way, it becomes alive, a part of you – but of a different you, an altogether *new* you. The mask and you combine to become something neither of you was before.

The Balinese are quick to interpret this psychological phenomenon as a sacred power that inhabits the mask. And with many of the masks representing gods, and the head considered the most sacred part of the body, the special status of masks in Bali is assured.

Masks are mostly made at Mas and Singapadu out of the wood of the *pule*, the tree called in Australia the milky pine.

TAKE-AWAY SHRINES

Carved stone is everywhere in Bali. Boss-eyed monsters with lolling tongues and long fangs cohabit happily with figures on flowery motorbikes, and there are not only no temples but few public buildings or private houses that don't boast at least some examples of the art.

Stone-carving is unlike wood-carving in that Western stylistic influence has been minimal, though figures from nature, as opposed to mythology, have long been incorporated into the designs. And Balinese wit, with wry comments on modern fashions, is everywhere.

Balinese temple stone-carvings – a sense of humor is frequently on show, while some happily display eroticism in the Hindu tradition. Stone-carving is one of the cheaper art forms to acquire, and almost all Balinese homes display some examples.

Stone-carvings also differ from wood-carvings in that the ordinary Balinese can afford to buy them. Prices are often very low, as little as Rp5,000 for the smallest pieces. The only problem for the visitor is weight – even so, little items a few centimeters high are on sale, and of just about any animal, bird, mythological or fanciful character you could wish for.

Almost all Balinese stone-carving goes on at Batubulan, home of the tourist version of the *barong* dance and on the road from Denpasar to Gianyar. Shops and workshops are one and the same, and all prices are negotiable.

The stone carved is a very soft sandstone, extremely easy to work but very friable. So pack your purchases carefully when taking them home, and remember they'll weather fast if kept outdoors. For some people, though, the temptation to have a mock-Balinese shrine in their garden will be understandably irresistible.

ENDEK, IKAT AND BATIK

Weaving enthusiasts will be eager to seek out the local handmade cloth, endek, where a pattern has been dyed into the weft by tying it here and there with strips of plastic. The cloth is made on old European-style handlooms in small factories, and is sold for local consumption in markets all over Bali.

Ikat, a cloth for which *both* warp and weft have been prepattern-dyed, is produced and sold in the Bali Aga village of Tenganan. It's an appallingly complex and time-consuming procedure, and you naturally pay for this when you buy the finished product.

Most visitors, however, will be content with the better-known batik from Java. Batik is not a Balinese product (though "Bali patterns" are always on offer) but both the brilliant "new" and the more delicately shaded "old" batik are on sale in all the main towns, and more or less everywhere that tourists frequent.

All three cloths are sold either direct from the bolt or made up into attractive, if not always very modern, articles of clothing.

GOLD AND SILVER

Despite the claims on the front of shops in Celuk, the center for gold in Bali is a small area of Denpasar, at the junction of Jalan Sulawesi and Jalan Hasanudin. Here items of jewelry are sold by weight, prices fol-

low the current price of gold, and the shops cater primarily to rich Balinese rather than to visitors.

Celuk, just past Batubulan coming out from Denpasar on the way to Gianyar or Ubud, is the silverware center. Intricately worked items – anything from rings to tableware – are a specialty, the smaller pieces virtually solid silver, the larger ones silver-plated. You can watch the silversmiths at work, and prices are very reasonable.

Balinese silverware – the subjects are usally sacred and the technique invariably superb. The center for silverware is the village of Celuk.

RIJSTTAFFEL TO *KRETEK*

FESTIVE FOODS

Humans, like animals, are astonishingly conservative where food is concerned. It seems that we learn to like what we are fed in childhood, modify this slightly by adventures in early adult life, and then stick to the limited repertoire we have acquired to the end of our days.

Consequently, Balinese food, being very different from what Westerners are used to, is unlikely to appeal to the average visitor anxious for the consolations of what he knows when he sits down to dinner after having been faced elsewhere with so much that was strange.

Besides, the local fare on ordinary days is very basic. Normal food for the Balinese is cold boiled or steamed rice *(nasi)* with a side dish of chopped and very highly spiced vegetables. This is prepared early in the day and left out, covered with squares of banana leaf, for members of the household to help themselves to whenever they feel hungry. It's eaten, with the right hand and preferably alone, on a banana-leaf plate that is then thrown to the pigs.

At festivals, however, far more complex dishes are prepared, and these, together with the tasty bits and pieces the Balinese love to eat at street stalls, are what the visitor is most likely to come across in the hotels and local restaurants. Only in the villages, or in the smaller eating places such as in Kuta's Night Market (see p.128), will you encounter the real thing.

Among these festive dishes, the best known is *be guling*, roast pork. It'll be marketed for you as *babi guling*, and you'll be told this means Balinese roast suckling pig. But the animal you'll be eating will have been three to six months old, and *babi* is

Sate is popular all over Indonesia. Here the tiny kebabs are waiting to be grilled on a street-side stall. They're usually eaten with a spicy peanut sauce.

anyway Indonesian, not Balinese. *Be* means meat and *guling* turned.

Next is *bebek betutu*, roast duck, the least difficult to come to terms with of the Balinese festival foods.

Thirdly, *lawar*, or *ebat*, is a mixture of raw, finely chopped meat (usually turtle or pig) and fruits and spices, endlessly grated down.

Of the humbler local dishes, *nasi goreng* (fried rice) is the commonest, and what most visitors, uncertain of what other options might imply, tend to fall back on. It can be anything from sumptuous to little more than greasy rice with the odd shrimp, egg and spring onion mixed in.

Nasi campur is another cheap filler, steamed rice with bits and pieces of everything on top. *Gado gado* is steamed beansprouts and vegetables, all under a sticky peanut sauce.

By contrast, the *rijsttaffel* was the Dutch colonial standby – a wide variety of different side-dishes served separately with steamed rice. It's usually ordered by a group, everyone taking what appeals to him.

Nasi padang is also a set of side dishes with rice, but it's true Indonesian (from the region of Padang in Sumatra), you can order only the things you fancy from a wide choice on the counter, and they all come highly spiced but cold.

Sate is a very popular Indonesian specialty, tiny kebabs – you usually order half a dozen or more – served with peanut or hot pepper sauce.

It won't be long before, having mastered some basic terms, you can begin to combine them, and recognize the combinations on menus. Thus, once you know chicken is *ayam*, coconut sauce *opor*, noodles *mee*, and bananas *pisang*, you won't have any problems identifying *ayam goreng* as fried chicken, *opor ayam* as chicken cooked in coconut sauce, *mee goreng* as fried noodles and *pisang goreng* as banana fritters. Rice cakes, the usual Balinese breakfast, are *jaja*.

On offer with virtually everything is *kecap*, not ketchup (though the pronunciation is identical) but soy sauce; *manis* is sweet, *asin* salty.

In the resort areas of Bali, Western food is as common as or commoner than Indonesian. Menus are self-explanatory – though perhaps non-Australians will need to be told that jaffles are toasted sandwiches sealed at the edges so that the contents come molten and gently bubbling.

DRINKS

Cold drinks assume a new and vital significance in the Balinese climate. Supreme among these must be the exquisite mixtures made everywhere, but specially delicious on beaches, of fresh fruit, ice, syrup and a dash of canned milk whisked together in a blender. They're called simply *es jus*, iced juice, and the going rate on Kuta Beach is Rp500 (Rp700 if they're brought to you where you're lying on the sand). You can choose any combination of the listed fruits, or else tell them to put in something of everything. These gorgeous drinks seem to *be* Bali. The silky property given them by a high proportion of avocado or papaya takes them within range of paradise itself.

Everything else is in a lower class, though the flavored yoghurt drink, *lassi*, isn't far behind.

For the rest, *air jeruk* is lemon (or orange) juice, made with fresh fruit, while *stroop* is fruit cordial.

Much has been written about the danger of taking ice in the tropics. The cogent argument is that if the water the ice was made from wasn't boiled, the ice will contain any infection that was present in the water. True, and a point worth remembering in many places. But for some years now the ice in Bali has been produced in approved factories and is, if not one hundred per cent safe, widely accepted.

Vividly colored rice-cakes (*jaja*, the most popular breakfast with the Balinese.

The ordinary tap water is NOT drinkable.

Commercially produced icecream is completely safe, but avoid the home-made variety peddled from street carts. Anything containing milk products needs careful handling and constant refrigeration in the tropics.

When it comes to alcohol, you are faced with the choice of rather expensive bottled products, similar to things you'll already know, and the very inexpensive local brews.

The latter are essentially three – *brem*, a very sweet wine made from black rice; *tuak*, a form of sweetish beer made from the sugar of the coconut palm; and *arak*, a deceptively tasteless brandy distilled from either *tuak* or *brem*. *Arak* and *brem* mixed is excellent.

As for non-Balinese intoxicants, imported wine is usually very dear and consequently not much drunk, spirits are available but dropped in favor of *arak* by many visitors, while beer comes in three brands, Bintang, San Miguel and Anker, all more or less excellent.

For the rest, tea is *teh* and coffee *kopi*. Each can be taken with milk (*susu*), and will come ready-sweetened unless you specifically request it without sugar, in which case add the word *tawar*. Thus coffee with milk but no sugar is *kopi susu tawar*.

TROPICAL FRUITS

The range of fruit available in Bali is almost a reason for going there in itself. Pineapples, papayas, coconuts, bananas, avocados – all are common and cheap. In addition there are a number of fruits you might be encountering for the first time – don't let this be a reason for not giving them a try. You don't want to find yourself tasting them for the first time on your last day and discovering, too late, that you were made for each other.

The following are the main attractions:

Salak – with a texture not unlike a Brazil nut but tasting like a lychee.

Rambutan – very like a lychee but with a hairy red skin.

Mangosteen – a fruit that travels badly and so is little known outside the tropics. The outside is black, brown or purple, and the inside stunning.

Blimbing – you can eat all of this refreshing pale green or yellow fruit. When cut, its cross-section is a five-pointed star, hence its Anglo-Saxon name star fruit.

Jambu-sotong – guavas.

Markisah – passion fruit. You'll see them on sale in the mountains – you break them open and eat everything you find inside, seeds and all. Exquisite is the only word for them.

Nangka – jackfruit. So big you'll only want to buy a segment. You eat the yellow inner part and discard the white outer layer.

Pleasures you never knew you liked until you tried – ABOVE: jackfruit; OPPOSITE: *salak*. Both are available everywhere, along with many other delights such as mangosteen, durian, custard apples and mangoes.

Jeruk – the word refers to all citrus fruits, but the pomelo, or *jeruk bali*, is the commonest. It's like a grapefruit but bigger, and the taste is a lot sweeter. Lemons are *jeruk nipis*, ordinary oranges *jeruk manis*.

Durian – love it or loathe it, this is the infamous fruit that stinks, but tastes to some people like heaven. You can even get durian-flavored icecream – a good means of judging whether or not you want to brave the real thing.

There are many more. If you see them on sale, give them a try. If you're worried you don't know which part to eat, ask the tradesman – street sellers in Indonesia will normally do just about anything to encourage you to buy. Just ask him to open one up for you, and if you don't trust his standard of hygiene, buy a couple and give him one, then eat them in tandem.

COCONUT PALMS

The Balinese venerate the coconut. The tree is such a generous provider, and considered such a friend to man, that, when I asked one hotel worker whether people were ever killed by coconuts falling to the ground, he said the tree was so kind he was quite sure it would never happen.

The coconut palm provides oil for cooking and lamps, sweet water to drink, flesh to eat or to make "milk" from for use in cooking, wood for house building and furniture, leaves for offerings, the "palm cabbage" (just below the head) for food, and gum from its flower buds for palm beer *(tuak)*. Copra, the dried meat of the nut from which oil can easily be extracted, has been one of the main exports from the tropical belt for over a century.

The Balinese, too, sometimes find time to enjoy the beach. Their snacks, though very cheap, are an acquired taste. Note the fully-clad bathers. The Balinese have no tradition of sea-going, and until recent years the ordinary people tended to be afraid of the sea.

SALT IN THE WOUND

An insight into the realities of the Third World life among which the tourist will find himself is provided by the economics of the salt-making business.

Salt in Bali is made from seawater, a process involving the carrying of large amounts of water from the sea onto the sand, carrying the wet sand into vats, the water from the vats into troughs and the final sludge from the troughs into filtering baskets. It's a family business, and an average family will produce 25 kg of salt a day during the dry season. The day's salt, product of at least two adults' labor, is sold for a grand total that averages out at Rp950 – about US$0.60. During the rainy season they produce nothing at all.

BETEL

Often, in the Balinese countryside, you'll come across what seems at first a terrifying spectacle – an older woman with lips stained scarlet, black teeth, a bulge in one cheek, and dribbling what looks like blood.

This is merely someone indulging in the very ancient and widespread Asian habit of chewing betel.

It's actually a combination of three basic ingredients folded together inside a betel leaf. Together they form a mild stimulant, aid to digestion and antiseptic all in one. But what is extraordinary, though hardly surprising, is that the Balinese have made it into a symbol of the three persons of God – Brahma, Wisnu and Siwa – and it is inconceivable for any temple offering to be made that doesn't include at least one sample.

JAMU

Jamu is a quintessentially Indonesian product, a herbal medicine marketed

by a wide range of outlets, from teenage girls with ready-mixed concoctions on their backs doing the rounds in the early mornings to giant wholesalers and distributors of their patent, albeit traditional, medicines. Air Mancur is not an Indonesian domestic airline but the biggest name in this huge *jamu* trade.

The science of *jamu* originated from the central Javanese city of Solo, and virtually everyone connected with the industry is still Solonese.

Jamu's most celebrated claim is that it increases sexual potency. If you're interested in putting this claim to the test, and are not sure whether your Indonesian is up to explaining what you want in the local supermarket, try the itinerant vendors. They'll probably be round far too early for you even to catch sight of them, but everyone else in Bali is up around 4 am and your room boy will undoubtedly be able to procure you a foul-tasting glassful. It will cost you around Rp300 – US$0.18. At that price, it's probably worth a try.

KRETEK

The first scent the arriving visitor receives on walking from his plane over to Immigration at Denpasar Airport is of cloves. This is altogether appropriate for what were once known as the Spice Islands, but the reason for the aroma today is that chopped cloves constitute 50 percent of Indonesia's most popular type of cigarette, *kretek*.

They're big business, and not least for the Indonesian government. The great Eiseman (see BIBLIOGRAPHY), admittedly using rather old statistics, estimates income from the tobacco industry constitutes 80 percent of all the country's tax revenue. He further reveals that, in one of the biggest tobacco companies' largest factories, every *kretek* cigarette is – believe it or not – rolled by hand.

The powers unleashed by even a judicious dose of the immensely popular *jamu* are not to be underestimated. In a culture that places great store on virility, aids to manliness are understandably in demand.

The Broad Highway

WITH its high mountains and low-lying coastal plains, Bali divides itself naturally into surprisingly self-defining areas. Not all, however, are of equal interest to the visitor. We have consequently dealt with those districts of most historical or contemporary interest at some length, and considered West Bali and the off-shore islands more briefly under the heading OFF THE BEATEN TRACK. *The areas where most of the tourist accommodation is situated are in the southeastern corner – Sanur, Nusa Dua and Kuta. The East, the area around Ubud, and the mountain locations are popular either for day trips or for excursions with one or two overnight stops. The same applies to the district we begin with, North Bali, nowadays somewhat neglected but once the gateway through which all visitors arrived on the island.*

NORTH BALI

Northern Bali is in many ways distinct from the rest of the island. Whereas to the south the land falls away from the central mountains quite gently, creating the extensive fertile plains where most of the island's population lives, to the north the land drops more steeply to the coast, affording little easily cultivable ground. Temperatures, too, are slightly higher than in the south and the rainfall approximately half that of the southern plains.

Nevertheless, the very fact that the area is somewhat different is in itself an attraction. The abrupt descent of the land to the sea provides excellent views northward from temples perched on projecting spurs of land, the drier climate allows the cultivation of grapes, and the 7 km (4 3/8 miles) beach-resort strip immediately west of Singaraja provides fine snorkeling and a peaceful ambiance that is very much to some people's taste.

Nowadays it is southern Bali that gets all the attention. With Denpasar as the

island's administrative center, the airport at Tuban, and Kuta beach a mecca now that surfing has become the premier beach pleasure, the north hardly gets a look-in.

But it wasn't long ago that everything was based on Singaraja. When K'tut Tantri, the American expatriate who "went native," first established her glamorous and quickly famous international hotel at Kuta in the thirties, the site she chose was as far as it was possible to

be from the center of operations of the colonial Dutch. Singaraja was their power-base and capital, largely because they had subdued northern Bali long before they extended their control to the south. International liners used the northern port (they now dock at Padangbai) and almost all foreign visitors arrived there.

Almost everyone nowadays arrives in north Bali by road from Denpasar via Bedugul. The 15-seater buses, often

North Bali is remote from the rest of the island – poorer, hotter and quieter. There are few tourists and all the accommodation is simple.

forced to accommodate rather more than that number of passengers, leave from the Ubung terminus. The fare Denpasar-Singaraja is Rp1,500, and the journey takes two hours. Travelers should not plan to leave Denpasar too late – buses are frequent up to 5 pm but you should check in advance at Ubung if you want to leave in the early evening. There are no buses during the night. buses do not operate to set timetables; they are privately operated and depart when they have recruited a full complement of passengers.

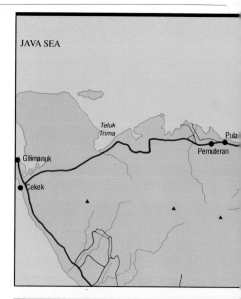

BALI'S OLD CAPITAL: SINGARAJA

Singaraja can seem an attractive enough place on a sunny morning, particularly from its upper streets commanding a view to the sea. But Bali is not a place that excels in its urban environments, and the truth is there is very little to see in the town. The library, **Gedong Kirtya**, is said to contain a collection of Balinese manuscripts, sacred and other texts inscribed on palm leaves (*lontar*), but no one I know has ever found the place open. The **Tourist Information Bureau**, next door to the library on Jalan Veteran, seems a superfluous institution and was understandably also closed the day I called.

Best is to see the town by night when the **Night Market** provides a dimly lit spectacle and adds a touch of glamor to a town that has little by day. When electricity is available, the market operates from 6 to 10 pm. On the frequent occasions when they have to make do with kerosene lamps things tend to end earlier. The many fruit sellers who set up at night along the main streets stay in business until midnight, however. One especially welcome feature of these stalls is the sale of apples, grown in the cooler mountain districts – to the embattled

The celebrated Pura Beji at Sangsit: "sublime cosmic harmonies have become modulated into beautifully wrought shapes of pinkish-colored stone".

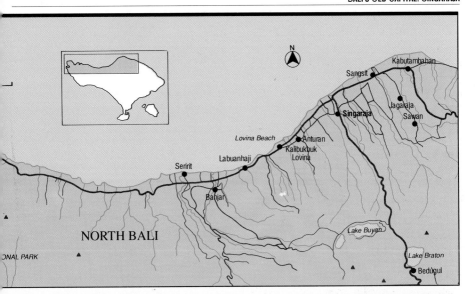

northerner suffering from a glut of tropical fruit, this is a blessing indeed. The market operates seven days a week, the two days of Nyepi (see THREE FESTIVALS, p.47) only excepted.

Virtually no foreign visitors actually stay in Singaraja as the attractive beachside *losmen* and hotels of Lovina are only a 15-minute bemo ride away. Anyone intent on spending a night in the northern capital, however, might try the **Ramayana Hotel** (© 41108; rates: moderate). Some rooms have air-conditioning.

BLACK-SAND BEACHES: LOVINA

Lovina is the general term covering the black-sand beaches that extend from just before Anturan village to the far end of Kalibukbuk, several kilometers to the west of Singaraja. There are virtually no local landmarks except for a prominent radio mast, clearly visible by day and night on the right of the road coming from Singaraja, and few buildings other than the beach hotels. All of these hotels, however, are well known to the bemo drivers coming out from the town – just name the place you plan to stay in and you will be dropped off near enough at the door.

Where to Stay

The following is a selection of the accommodation available. There are some forty places in all, clearly too many for the interested market. We looked at a good many and found these to be satisfactory or better. All accommodation at Lovina can be assumed to be from a third to a half cheaper than its equivalent at beaches in the southeast of the island.

East to west, the **Baruna Beach Inn** (© 41252; rates: inexpensive) is simple with attractive, rather unusual rooms, and right on the beach. It is not one of the smarter hotels, but boasts a conference center capable of seating three hundred people, a rarity, not to say an oddity, in this part of the world. The **Suci Jati Reef**

(© 21952; rates: moderate) consists of some newly built bungalows between the rice paddies and the beach; it is still in the process of development and a restaurant is being added. The **Janur Dive Inn** – also known as John's Dive Inn – (rates: inexpensive) is a very friendly, relaxed place reflecting the jolly personality of its owner; students might well feel at home here. By contrast the **Banyualit Beach Inn** (© 41889; rates: moderate) is one of the most luxurious places in Lovina, with its own power generator in case of the inevitable power failures and even air-conditioning in two of its 14 bungalow-type rooms. All rooms have bedside telephone extensions.

All of the above are situated before the radio mast when coming from Singaraja. After the mast you have the Astina and the Ayodya, two attractive places under one management. The **Astina** (rates : inexpensive) is on the beach and like many another beach hotel; the **Ayodya** (rates: inexpensive) is unlike anywhere else in Bali. Its attractions are those of a colonial country house in the tropics at the beginning of the century. Writers and philosophers, you feel, would be very happy here.

A little further on is the **Nirwana**, an excellent place right on the beach with a pleasantly situated coffee shop (rates: inexpensive). Further west again you come to the **Aditya** (© 21781; rates: moderate), a stylish place with a restaurant and even a shop. Lastly, the **Parma Beach Homestay** (rates: inexpensive) is simple, colorful, and serves large portions of homely food.

It should be noted that *all* the accommodation at Lovina is relatively unsophisticated, certainly by the standards of Sanur or Nusa Dua. Many of the places are still waiting to be connected to the telephone and there is nowhere to go at night other than to the other hotels or one of the few restaurants. Notable among these are the unexpected **Hungarian Restaurant** and the **Nirwana Restaurant** – distinct from the beach-side hotel – both of them in **Kalibukbuk** village. All the hotels, however, offer snorkeling equipment for hire and boats out the short distance to the reef.

Many, though by no means all, of the hotels and *losmen* not listed here have an abandoned and even derelict look to them, and one or two seem like the end of the world. A couple seem to be in the process of reverting to the role of rural villages, no tourists having stayed there perhaps within

the sea, it is the home for getting on for a hundred monkeys. Don't imagine, though, that you're doing them a favor when you buy them nuts from the ever-ready vendors – every local farm vehicle that passes empties out sackfuls of fruit oddments for them onto the road, an operation that makes the temple an inevitable slowing-down point for all traffic. It's in the nature of a religious offering, just as when bemo drivers pull up at shrines – no one is getting off, but the

living memory. But maybe even these have their own weird attraction. The best places, though, the Nirwana, the Banyualit and the Aditya, should give no cause whatever for complaint.

SPRINGS AND TEMPLES

North Bali has several attractions besides those of the beach (which are limited, anyway, to the pleasures of snorkelling and underwater photography).

Fifty-six kilometers (35 miles) west from Singaraja on the coast road to Gilimanuk there is the **Pulaki Monkey Temple**. Sited on the road overlooking

conductor *(kernet)* jumps down and places a tiny wicker tray of flowers and food there. The monkeys of Pulaki, sitting as often as not all over the road eating grapes and chunks of pineapple, are happy beings on the receiving end of the same pious devotion.

The Hot Springs at **Banjar**, 18 km (11 1/4 miles) west of Singaraja, is one of the nicest places in the north. Whereas before 1985 there were only muddy pools fed by

---

Black sand, fishing nets, the shore serving as a major footpath - the lonely coast of North Bali. There is little to do at night but eat and sleep, and dream of the next day's snorkeling.

water falling through bamboo pipes, now there is a modern complex worthy, albeit on a small scale, of Budapest or Baden-Baden. There are two tiled pools, one set above the other, into which a warm and slightly sulfurous stream of water gushes through magnificent dragon (*naga*) mouths. There is a restaurant up above, and the whole ambiance, with its flowering shrubs and terraced garden overlooking the baths, is utterly delightful. It's rather like coming across the Emperor Nero's private retreat right in the middle of a tropical jungle.

To get there, ask the bemo driver for *air panas* at Banjar. You will be put down at a road junction where several horse-drawn traps (*dokar*) will be waiting to take you the 2 km (1 1/4 mile) drive up to the village (fare: Rp200). From there, a broad path leads off to the left, and 15 minutes' walk past rice paddies will bring you to the springs. It's impossible to get lost, but someone will take you on a motorbike if you ask (you will have to negotiate the fare). You can even go by motorbike all the way from the main road.

A privately negotiated ride on the back of a bike is also the best way to get from the springs to the **Buddhist Temple**, Banjar's other attraction and something not to be missed. It's a walk through jungle of under a kilometer but it seems it's possible to lose your way; the motorbikes go by the road the long way round. (Rp500 for the one-way trip would be generous).

The temple is a beautiful mixture of Buddhist and Balinese Hindu elements. Set on a steep hill overlooking the sea, it contains a lily pond, a yellow Buddha and numerous red-tiled roofs at different levels that make a most attractive combination. It's an easy walk back down to the coast road.

The falls at **Labuanhaji** are of less interest. A river forces its way through a cleft in the rocks and falls some 6 m (19 1/2 ft) into a murky pool. There is another fall and pool above, accessible by a slippery path.

Whereas it's certain that after heavy rain these waterfalls would be more impressive, nevertheless, given their modest scale and the lack of any facilities (in contrast to Banjar), they are barely worth the 1 1/2 km (7/8 mile) trudge from the road. If you do go, boys will press their services on you as "guides," in effect showing you where to turn off the lane and take the short brick path beside the paddy.

UNHEARD MELODIES

Eight kilometers (5 miles) east of Singaraja is the celebrated **Pura Beji** at **Sangsit**. It is one of the most elaborately carved temples in all Bali, so much so that carved wings stand right out, all but free from the mother stone.

In the clammy silence, the smiling faces of the men and gods gaze out in voluptuous ease, caught forever in a moment of serene resignation. The peace and infinite generosity of Balinese Hinduism is wonderfully expressed here in this gorgeous place. "Heard melodies are sweet," wrote the English poet Keats,

"but those unheard are sweeter." Here at Pura Beji the most sublime cosmic harmonies have become modulated into beautifully wrought shapes of pinkish-colored stone.

The temple is not difficult to find. A small sign points the way downhill off Sangsit's main street, but anyone will show you the way – it's the only place in this little agricultural market any visitor ever goes to.

GONGS

Sawan, another 9 km (5 5/8 miles) east, is a most attractive village. It's known as the place where gongs for *gamelan* orchestras are fired – just say "gong" and any child will lead you up a lane and through a barn door, and there they will be, a couple of men and a woman hammering, polishing and working bellows for the fire.

But the real charm lies in just wandering through this very restful place, taking lunch at a street-side *warung*, and watching the easy, tranquil village life walk by. Sawan is reached by bemo from the main

road between Sangsit and Kubutambahan, passing the village of **Jagaraga** on the way up (fare: Rp300).

The temple at **Kubutambahan** is at the junction of the road down from Kintomani and the coast road. Most visitors give the place only a couple of minutes – time enough to photograph the carving of a man on a flowery bicycle: the guardian will show you where it is once you have signed the visitors' book and paid your donation.

YEH SANIH

At Yeh Sanih, another 6 km (3 3/4 miles) east, freshwater springs have been diverted to create bathing pools between the road and the sea. There's an accompanying restaurant and accommodation, **Bungalow Puri Sanih** (rates: inexpensive). Frogs croak, mosquitoes bite, and boys flop into the cool water.

The coast, as elsewhere in north Bali, has a rather bleak appearance. The bungalow rooms are satisfactory, and there's a small temple up a short path on the other side of the road. You might be lucky when you visit it to hear a strange and beautiful whistling and tinkling in the air – a few members of a local bird orchestra out for a quick run-through of a small part of their repertoire.

VILLAGE WITH A VIEW

Sembiran is a large village 3 km (1 7/8 miles) up from the road. The road is good, but transport is by motorbike – a group of them wait at the junction for prospective customers (Rp500 should be considered a maximum fare).

The village itself is rather neglected though was clearly once important. Visitors are few, and children run away startled

OPPOSITE and ABOVE: the Buddhist temple at Banjar. Buddhist elements coexist with the dominant Hinduism without abrasion – there are, for example, Buddhist *pedanda* (high priests) as well as Hindu ones.

as you approach. What is very fine about Sembiran, though, is the **temple** perched on the hillside 1 km (5/8 mile) before you get to the village proper. Your transport will wait for you while you take a couple of pictures, but don't linger too long as other fares are waiting and he will not be slow to urge you on. Best, perhaps, is to walk back down from the village (the temple will be on your left) and inspect it at your leisure.

Characteristically of north Bali, the site commands an excellent view out over the sea, though technically, like all Balinese temples, it is oriented upwards to the mountains. Trimly kept, the place has an almost Greek atmosphere, and its gray stone and green grass give it a simplicity which is classical.

SANUR

A DISCREET CAMPARI

Sanur is altogether a very comfortable place – not cheap, but long-established, leafy and reassuring. The beach may not be up to Kuta's but then no beach in Bali is. You are in Indonesia, just about, when you are in Sanur, whereas in Nusa Dua further south, despite all their attempts to prove the contrary, you could be on the moon.

All the hotels, except the Bali Beach Hotel and the Bali Hyatt, are of the bungalow type and set in shady tropical gardens, most of them fronting onto the beach. And the beach is safe, has yellow sands and colorful fishing boats, is sheltered behind a reef where snorkeling is available, and has a fine view east with the mountains of central Bali rising grandly across the bay.

All the tourist facilities available in such profusion in Kuta are here too, but presented in a more genteel, affluent way. Sanur is a lush garden where visitors lie on beach beds under palm trees sipping their Camparis or flop splendidly into a pool. (Hotels without pools can't really compete

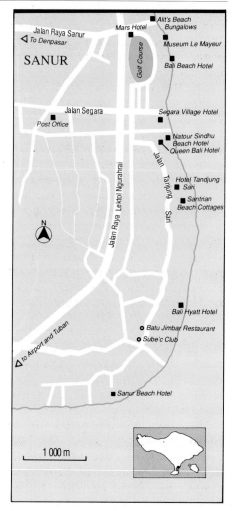

in Sanur.) Leather traveling bags replace canvas ones. It's as discreet and worldly wise as Kuta is fresh and brash and innocent. You pay your money – rather more than in Kuta, but less than in Nusa Dua – and you take your choice.

WHERE TO STAY

Almost all the more exclusive hotels in Sanur are right on the beach. Starting from the north and working south, you'll come across **Alit's Beach Bungalows** ((© 8567 and 8560; 98 rooms; rates: average and above). The hotel is situated where the continuation of the road from Denpasar arrives at the sea. Just carry straight on after the traffic lights, leaving the grand entrance to the grounds of the Bali Beach Hotel on your right. All rooms have air-con and hot running water and there is a swimming pool.

The **Bali Beach Hotel** (© 8511; 605 rooms; rates: expensive) probably has every facility anyone is likely to require. It's the only hotel outside Nusa Dua built upwards rather than in the more usual bungalow/garden style, but it also has its low-rise wing and cottages. You approach the hotel down a long drive with a nine-hole golf-course on the right, where figures in white tropical suits swing their clubs with Balinese caddies in attendance. A *gamelan* orchestra celebrates your arrival for lunch, and many of the airlines are in the process of establishing offices in the hotel to facilitate your smooth departure.

The **Segara Village Hotel** (© 8407/8 and 8231; 100 rooms; rates: expensive) has two-story cottages in garden surroundings, is quiet and relaxing, and also fronts onto the beach. It has special programs and facilities for children.

Two slightly less expensive hotels, the **Natour Sindhu Beach Hotel** (© 8351/2; 50 rooms; rates: average and above) and the **Queen Bali Hotel** (© 8054; rates: average and above) are situated close together either on the sea front or, in the case of the Queen Bali, a few paces away.

Continuing south, the **Hotel Tandjung Sari** (© 8441; 25 rooms; rates: expensive) is the preferred hideaway for celebrities and jet-setters in Sanur. For many it is *the* place to stay in Bali. Meanwhile the **Santrian Beach Cottages** (© 8009; 75 rooms; rates: average and above) offer the usual one-and two-story bungalows in the usual verdant tropical gardens.

The **Bali Hyatt** (© 8271; 387 rooms; rates: expensive), set in an astonishing 15 hectares (36 acres) of land, combines very Balinese public areas with four-story accommodation. High thatched roofs rise over restaurants serving food from Indonesia and Italy, and sauna and disco complete the international-yet-in-Bali ambiance.

Lastly, at the far end of the beach the **Sanur Beach Hotel** (© 8011; 346 rooms; rates: expensive) is the friendliest of the big Sanur hotels. It's recently been renovated and is usually booked solid by tour groups.

As you might except, the cheaper accommodation tends to be back from the beach, but it's never very far. Sanur does not specialize in facilities for budget travelers, but the **Mars Hotel** (© 8236; 12 rooms; rates: moderate) in the north and the **Taman Agung Inn** (© 8549; 18 rooms; rates: moderate) to the south are among the handful of places in this category.

WHERE TO EAT

Sanur looks as if it teems with restaurants. This is because, like the hotels, they all crowd together along the one road running just inland from the beach, Jalan Tanjung Sari. There's the **Yuyu Restaurant** (© 8009) specializing in sea food; the inexpensive **Alita** that closes at 9 pm; the **Kesunasar** (© 8371; rates: moderate), a restaurant and pub; the **Italian Terrazzo Martini** (© 8371; rates: moderate); and **Ronny's Pub and Restaurant** (© 8370; rates: average and above) with live music Mondays, Thursdays and Saturdays.

The **Karya Bar and Restaurant** (© 8376; rates: average and above) is one of Sanur's many stylish establishments. There's a choice of Italian, Chinese, Indonesian or international food with a Balinese dance show on Tuesdays, and live music on Wednesdays, Fridays and Sundays. Transport is provided from local hotels – just give them a ring. There's a Japanese restaurant, too, the **Kita** (© 8158; rates: average and above), serving, among other dishes, *sukiyaki*, *tempura* and *yakitori*. Note that it closes at 9:30 pm.

The further south you go in Sanur, once you're past the Hyatt, the cheaper it gets. After the road becomes a dirt track there are a number of very reasonable *warung*, bars and small restaurants to be found.

NIGHTLIFE

As for discos, the **Number One** at Batu Jumbar (the name for the southern end of Sanur) provides transport, free from Sanur hotels or Rp3,000 from Kuta. Phone them on 8097.

It's a smart place: no shorts, thongs (flip-flops) or singlets. Considering this is precisely the attire most holiday-makers in Bali wear all the time, this constitutes some requirement. There's also **Subec** on Jalan Tanjung Sari, and there's another disco in the **Bali Hyatt**.

SHOPPING

Souvenir and art shops of the classier kind are a feature of Sanur, and **Keramik Jenggala** at Batu Jimbar is an excellent place for pottery.

The **Mata Grafik Bookshop** on Jalan Tanjung Sari offers a range of new books at slightly more reasonable prices than the bookshops in the big hotels.

In addition, there are shopping arcades at the bigger Sanur hotels such as the Bali Hyatt and the Hotel Bali Beach. Prices here, however, are above those in many of the small shops elsehwhere on the island.

AN EXPLOSION OF PAINT

One of the few historical sites in Sanur is the house, now known as the **Museum Le Mayeur**, where the Belgian painter Le Mayeur lived from 1932 to 1958. The place has been left more or less as it was, with his books still on his desk and so on. What is so striking about the house is that his painting explodes from the framed pictures onto the walls and eventually all over the window frames. Fantastic scenes from the *Ramayana* epic in augmented Balinese style feature prominently. There are several rooms, and plans are afoot to restore the building before the effects of the tropical climate cause it to deteriorate still further.

It's the daughter of Le Mayeur's Balinese wife who shows you round, and she also runs the small establishment adjacent to the house called the **Pollok Art Shop**. This stocks a well-chosen mixture of items: silver jewelry, wood-carvings, batik, some paintings, T-shirts – a range that makes it possible to shop for souvenirs and presents all in the one place and avoid the need to tramp at length in the heat to different shops round the district.

BALI'S CAPITAL: DENPASAR

Denpasar is emphatically not an attractive place. It is Bali's capital, but few tourists have any need to go there, or any good reports of it once they've been and escaped back to Kuta or Sanur to tell the tale. There are, for instance, numerous small hotels and *losmen* there, but it's rare that anyone other than Indonesians from outside Bali on business in Denpasar stays in them.

It's a crowded, noisy, polluted town, the very antithesis of everything people come to Bali to find. Like many another Asian city, it's caught between two moments in history; it was built for an age of horse-drawn or pedestrian traffic and now

Tourists enjoying a ride on a *prahu* off Sanur.

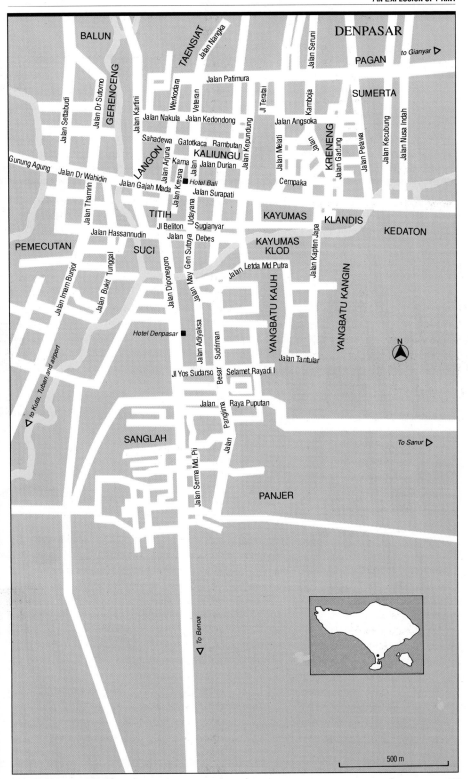

BALUN

TAENSIAT

Jalan Nangka

DENPASAR

Jalan Seruni

PAGAN

to Gianyar ▷

GERENCENG

Jalan Dr Sutomo

Jalan Settabudi

Jalan Kartini

Jalan Patimura

Werkodara

Veteran

SUMERTA

Jalan Nakula

Jalan Kedondong

JI Teratai

Jalan Angsoka

Kamboja

Jalan Kecubung

Jalan Pelawa

Jalan Nusa Indah

Sahadewa

Gatotkaca

Rambutan

KALIUNGU

Jalan Melati

KRENENG

Jalan

Jalan Gadung

Gunung Agung

Jalan Dr Wahidin

LANGON

Karna

Jalan Arjuna

Jalan Durian

Jalan Kepundung

Jalan Thamrin

Jalan Gajah Mada

Jalan Kresna

Hotel Bali ■

Jalan Surapati

Cempaka

TITIH

Udayana

Jalan Beliton

Sugianyar

KAYUMAS

KLANDIS

KEDATON

Jalan Hassannudin

Jalan

Debes

KAYUMAS
KLOD

Jalan Bukit Tunggal

PEMECUTAN

SUCI

Jalan Diponegoro

Jalan May Gen Sutoya

Jalan Letda Md Putra

Jalan Kapten Japa

YANGBATU KAUH

YANGBATU KANGIN

N

Jalan Imam Bunjol

Hotel Denpasar ■

Jalan Adiyaksa

Sudirman

Jalan Tantular

To Kuta, Tuban and airport ▽

JI Yos Sudarso

Besar

Selamet Rayadi I

Jalan

Raya Puputan

SANGLAH

Jalan Panglima

To Sanur ▷

Jalan Serma Md. Pii

PANJER

To Benoa ▽

500 m

endures the full force of modern mechanized transport.

So great is the tourist concentration in Kuta and Sanur that even shopping and such services as banks, telex offices and travel agents are as good there as in Denpasar, or better. A visit to the Immigration Office, or the Denpasar Police Office to get a license to drive a motorbike on Bali if you don't have an international driver's license, is the most likely reason for paying a visit to the town.

Nevertheless, Denpasar does have one or two places of interest and these will be dealt with briefly here.

HEROIC LAST STAND

The center of Denpasar can be said to be a large grassy square known as the **Tanah Lapang Puputan Badung**. Its only notable feature is a heroic, three-figure statue standing in pools unfortunately empty and with their fountains defunct. As a memorial to the four thousand Balinese who died defending the city against the Dutch

Eyes of tourist and local alike are turned seaward. Sanur.

on September 20, 1906 it deserves better treatment.

Standing facing the monument from the center of the square, the building on your right is the **Museum Bali**, with the Pura Jagatnatha next to it on the left. Over on the opposite side of the square is the military headquarters for the island.

Frankly, for a place with the cultural significance of Bali, the museum is a bit of a joke. The basic concept, that its very buildings should in themselves be exhibits of Balinese temple and palace architectural styles, is attractive. But unfortunately the contents have neither the range, nor are they labeled clearly and in sufficient languages, to make them the major resource such an institution really ought to house.

Exhibits include a model of a tooth-filing ceremony, some interesting masks, some paintings and wood-carvings and a display of agricultural tools and implements. There is no catalog available in English.

Entry to the museum is Rp200, children Rp100. Opening hours are from 8 am to 2 pm daily, except for Fridays when the museum closes at 11 am, and Mondays when it is closed all day.

The **Pura Jagatnatha** is a modern temple dedicated to the whole of Bali. Unlike most Balinese temples, it is closed to the public except at festival times.

ART AND INFORMATION

Two art centers provide useful indications of what riches the island has in store. The **National Art Center**, between Jalan Abiankapas and Jalan Palawa Pagan in the east of the town, contains exhibits of shadow puppets and the giant *barong landong* puppets, silverware, carvings, basketry, paintings and weaving. Further east – you'll need to take a taxi – is the government-run, fixed-price art shop; ask the driver for **Sanggraha Kriya Asta**. It not only has a wide range of items but it also provides a convenient indication of the kind of prices to be paid for similar objects elsewhere when you will be expected to bargain for them.

You can attend lessons in Balinese dance at two places in Denpasar. One is the **Academy of Dance, Indonesia** (otherwise known as ASTI) on Jalan Nusa Indah. The other is the **Conservatory of Performing Arts** (otherwise known as KOKAR) – check with the Badung Tourist Office for the location of this one as they were about to move at the time of writing. Lessons at each institution take place in the mornings.

There is a six-week long annual **Bali Arts Festival** between mid-June and the end of July at the Werdi Budaya Arts Center, Jalan Nusa Indah.

The **Badung Government Tourist Office** at Merdeka Building, 7 Jalan Surapati (℗ 23399 and 23602), provides maps, lists of festivals (valuable as these go by the Balinese calendar and so vary from year to year) and details of dance and other performances. It's not the full service provided by some countries but the attendants are helpful and do respond to personal inquiries. The office is open from 7 am to 2 pm daily, except on Friday when it closes at 11 am and Monday when it is shut all day.

The **Bali Government Tourist Office**, by contrast, is difficult to find, being located in a complex of government buildings, and not really oriented to the needs of the individual inquirer. If, however, you think you need them, they're at Jalan S. Parman, Niti Mandala Renon (℗ 22387 and 26313).

Should you happen to hold a visa of the kind that can be renewed (see TRAVELERS' TIPS for information on visas), then you may need to go to the **Immigration Office**. It's at Jalan Diponegoro 222 (℗ 2439). It's open from 7 am to 1 pm, except on Friday when it closes at 11 am, Saturday when it closes at 12 noon, and Sunday when it's shut.

WHERE TO STAY

If you need for any reason to stay in Denpasar, one of the following should suit your needs. The best hotel in town is the **Bali Hotel** (℗ 5681/5; 73 rooms; rates: average and above). It's the old Dutch colonial hotel, and though now over fifty years old it has been tastefully modernized, and has a swimming pool and an ambiance that manages to be both efficient and relaxed. It's located at Jalan Veteran 3. And you might be surprised at the lineage of some of your fellow guests at the **Pamecutan Palace,** (℗ 23491, 44 rooms, rates: average and above, at Jalan Thamrin 2. Then there's the **Hotel Denpasar** (℗ 26363 and 26336; 65 rooms; rates: moderate) with a variety of types of room from air-conditioned, self-contained cottages to inexpensive plain rooms with a ceiling fan. Special rates are available for students. It's at Jalan Diponegoro 103.

A smaller, homely place is the **Wismasari Inn** (℗ 22437; 14 rooms; rates: moderate) at Jalan Majen Sutoyo 1. Rooms are very clean and reasonably comfortable.

WHERE TO EAT

Food in Denpasar tends to be Indonesian as foreign tourists are not that common. The Bali Hotel, however, provides a varied cuisine, and the small and tourist-oriented **Puri Selera Restaurant** (rates: moderate) on Jalan Gajah Mada offers well-prepared Indonesian and Chinese food in hygienic surroundings. It's open 7 am to 5 pm on weekdays and closed on Sundays.

SHOPPING

Most of Denpasar's major shops are situated on Jalan Gajah Mada, but if you're using public transport you'll have to walk there as bemos are not allowed to drive along it. A selection of books on Bali in English can be seen at the **Corsica Bookshop** on Jalan Sumatra.

TRANSPORT

There are three main bemo stations in Denpasar, **Tegal**, **Ubung** and **Kereneng**. Little three-wheel bemos shuttle back and forth between them for a couple of hundred rupiah a ride. Tegal serves Kuta, the airport, Ulu Watu and Nusa Dua (should anyone staying at Nusa Dua ever want to use a bemo). Ubung, somewhat out of town, serves the west and north; minibuses leave from here to Gilimanuk and Singaraja. Kereneng is the station for services to Sanur, Ubud, Kintamani and east Bali.

There are two other small terminals, for Benoa Port and Sangeh (the Monkey Forest), at **Suci** and **Wangaya** respectively.

One final point – all over Bali you will hear bemo drivers touting for passengers calling out *"Badung!"* In fact, *"Badung, Badung!"* rings through the dusty evening air from Klungkung to Kuta, from Ubud to Tabanan. You won't find it on any map, but just as Karangasem is the old Balinese name for Amlapura, and Buleleng for Singaraja, Badung is the name by which all Balinese know the Denpasar area, and these tired and hungry drivers are looking for their last fares of the day before finally heading home.

NUSA DUA AND THE BUKIT

IN PRAISE OF LIMESTONE

The region south of the airport is generally referred to as the Bukit. It is the Balinese word for hill and strictly refers only to the high ground southwest of Nusa Dua. Nevertheless, the whole peninsula is of a piece, and the reason is that whereas the rest of mainland Bali is made up of volcanic rock and soils, the Bukit, like the nearby offshore island of Nusa Penida, is entirely limestone. Indeed, it is probable that at one time the Bukit was once an island too: even today it is only connected to Bali proper by a low-lying and rather narrow isthmus.

Rainwater runs straight into the ground in limestone country, and the consequent lack of surface streams means there is no water available for irrigation during the dry season. As a result, in the Bukit life has traditionally been hard. The selection of Nusa Dua (literally Two Islands) for development as a major tourist complex has done little to alter the traditional life of the region.

The area includes the five-star complex of Nusa Dua itself, the fishing village of Tanjung Benoa sited at the end of a five kilometer sand strip directly to the north of Nusa Dua), the village and bay of Jimbaran (located on the neck of the isthmus immediately south of the airport) and the upland area itself that culminates in the magnificently sited temple and surfing venues of Ulu Watu.

FIVE-STAR ONLY

The development of Nusa Dua only really got under way in the early eighties. Prior to that, the area was an infertile coastal patch featuring the two small "islands," connected to the mainland by sandy strips, which give the place its name.

There can be no doubt about the magnificence of the hotels, all of them five-star, at Nusa Dua. All come up to the highest international standards and stand in their own ample grounds complete with several restaurants, swimming pools, etc. Indeed, each of them is a self-sufficient holiday environment, and anything that might be thought to be missing – Balinese local culture, for instance – is brought in and presented for the hotel guests' exclusive delectation. Whether this really adds up to what you expect from a vacation in Bali is, in the last analysis, a matter for you to decide.

Outside the hotels themselves, Nusa Dua is perhaps something less than first-class. The beaches, though of white sand,

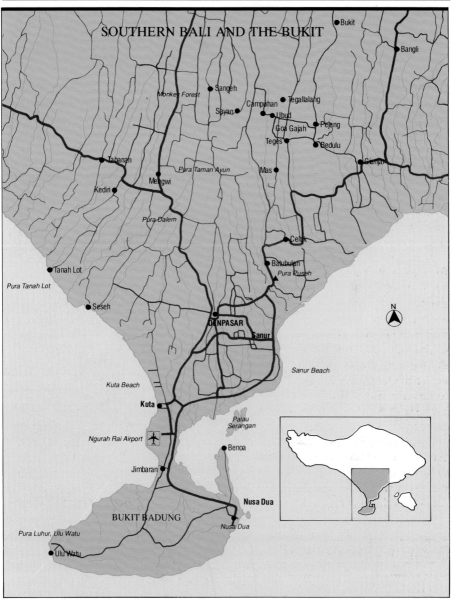

SOUTHERN BALI AND THE BUKIT

are not the best on the island; something of their tameness derives from your not being very likely to meet anyone other-than people staying or working at the Nusa Dua hotels. To some people, however, this is a positive advantage, and certainly anyone concerned about security can be confident that here they are staying in a place specially designed with their safety in mind. Along the long avenues of palms that link the access roads to

the hotels, security men are stationed on-their motorbikes, lolling in boredom across the handlebars of their machines. Their main function in normal times seems to be to keep hawkers away from-these wide acres in which are concentrated many of the richest people staying on Bali at any one moment.

The atmosphere created by well-trimmed verges and impeccable tarred driveways is more that of a presidential golf-course than somewhere given over to free-and-easy relaxation. And indeed the **Nusa Dua Beach Hotel** (© 71210; 450 rooms; rates: expensive) is where heads of state stay when they visit Indonesia, government officials flying down from Jakarta to meet them here rather than having to face the security nightmare presented by the nation's capital. The Reagans stayed there, in a presidential suite "with special security features," in 1986, and in many ways the whole district,

big, traditional hotel at Nusa Dua. The name means "Balinese Princess."

The **Bali Club Med** (© 971520-5; 350 rooms; rates: expensive) is rather different. In common with the other "clubs" in the chain, the vacation offered is more organized that most, so that few decisions are left to the "gentle members" and an atmosphere of group pleasure is cultivated. Access to the hotel by outsiders is permitted at certain hours, but the procedures for gaining it do tend to resemble

with access confined to a narrow bottleneck close to the airport, is ideal for such uses. Nusa Dua as a whole was conceived as an environment in which world statesmen could meet, and tourists subsequently pay for the honor of breathing the air of the same prestigious environment.

The architectural style of the Nusa Dua Beach Hotel is solidly generous, while its rooms are in four-story blocks. The **Bali Sol** (© 71510; 500 rooms; rate: expensive), by contrast, mixes tropical and Spanish styles in its conception; it too has rooms in four-story blocks.

The **Putri Bali** (© 71020 and 71420; 425 rooms; rates: expensive) is the other

those for visiting the inmates of a psychiatric hospital.

The smallest of Nusa Dua's hotels is the **Hotel Bualu** (© 71310; 50 rooms; rates: expensive). It is particularly suited to vacations with children for whom supervised activities are provided. It is also the only hotel in Indonesia for PADI (Professional Association of Diving Instructors) scuba diving. The Bualu is adjacent to a training school for students studying the tourism business, and students undertake periods of work in the hotel as a part of their course. An unusually large number of sporting facilities, such as for riding and sailing, are provided free of charge.

The Nusa Dua complex as a whole has a wide variety of leisure facilities on tap centrally located for the use of guests at all five hotels.

UNEXPECTED BENOA

Benoa is actually the name for the port of Denpasar; the fishing village that faces it from the other side of the bay is Tanjung Benoa. It's a longish way round from one to the other by road, but a short trip by boat. Between the two, sheltering the entrance to the bay, lies Pulau Serangan, commonly known to tour operators as Turtle Island.

It is the fishing village that's most likely to interest visitors. It's an unexpected place, slightly down-market with a raffish, freewheeling air, like somewhere long forgotten but determined to stand up for itself. The truth is probably that the development of Nusa Dua 5 km (3 1/8 miles) to the south has seen a considerable improvement in the village's prosperity. It is certainly an excellent base for a wide variety of water sports, a jumping-off point for trips to Pulau Serangan, and the location of two very fine restaurants.

Sea, Sun and Food

Diving, parasailing, scuba diving, snorkeling, wind surfing and water skiing – all these can be arranged from operators working out of the two major restaurants in the village, the Mentari and the Rai.

Both are excellent places and it isn't really possible to recommend one rather than the other. The **Rai Seafood Restaurant** (rates: average and above) has a cocktail bar and fresh seafood daily. The **Mentari Bar and Restaurant** (© 8556 and 8691; rates: average and above) also has a well-stocked bar and offers Indonesian and Western food, and there is even a Japanese dish on the menu, *teriyaki ginza*. Both places have wonderful late-afternoon views across the strait to the cliffs on the south side of Nusa Penida. They are actually situated side by side, and, if you fancy a meal in one of them and don't know which to choose, nothing could be easier than to have a drink in each and make your choice afterwards. Whichever one you eat in, you're unlikely to come away unsatisfied.

Benoa is a very attractive place to spend a day in and around. It's that rather unusual thing in Bali, somewhere that is still very Indonesian and

yet contains sophisticated establishments geared toward what most tourists are interested in. Lunch at one of the restaurants followed by an afternoon pottering round the fishing boats on the shore, inspecting the recently renovated Chinese temple, and then finally crossing over for a look at Pulau Serangan would yield interesting and rather untypical Bali experiences, plus some

OPPOSITE: the Nusa Dua Hotel, one of the handful of five-star hostelries in this ultra-exclusive enclave; all have international-standard facilities as well as sharing some sporting amenities. ABOVE: a young celebrant heads home after a festival; Mas.

unusual photographs, commercialized though Turtle Island has undoubtedly become. And then, of course, you could always visit the restaurant you didn't opt to eat lunch in and sample all their specialties on your return journey.

TURTLE ISLAND

Pulau Serangan (Turtle Island) is a low, sandy spit only cut off from the mainland to the north at high tide. Variations in tidal levels, however, make it inadvisable to cross other than by boat. The island is covered by palm trees and at its one village turtles are kept in pens being fattened up for sale on the "mainland." You can charter a small boat to take you across from either the northern or southern side – from the southern, Nusa Dua side the cost is likely to be around Rp7,000 there and back per boatload, with room for several people. The island is a popular destination for half-day tours from Kuta and you'll probably have a nicer time if you plan your trip to avoid coinciding with one of these – early in the morning, say, or at the end of the afternoon.

A FISHING BEACH

The village of **Jimbaran** straddles the road running south from close by the airport to Ulu Watu. It is not in itself remarkable, but just after you pass the stalls of the village market a road leaves off to the right where some very tall *kepuh* trees mark the site of a cemetery where bodies awaiting cremation are buried. A prominent sign indicates this is the way to the Pan Sea Puri Bali Hotel.

After a few hundred meters you arrive at **Jimbaran Bay**. This is a most attractive white-sand beach some 2 km (1 1/4 miles) wide. At the northern (right-hand) end, the airport runway can be seen, with the planes standing silhouetted against the sky. Between you and the airport a couple of dozen fishing boats will almost certainly be pulled up on the beach.The sands run

away again to the left until they reach a green headland, while immediately on your left is the hotel.

The **Hotel Puri Bali** (℡ 25442; 41 rooms; rates: average and above) is right on the beach and accommodation is in air-conditioned bungalow-type rooms. This small hotel seems to combine personal service with modern comforts; it virtually has a big beach to itself, yet also provides a free shuttle service to Kuta three times a day. For an excellent **guide service** covering this area, or indeed any other part of Bali, contact I. Wayan Budiasa by leaving a message for him here. Alternatively, his mailing address is: PO Box 1035, Denpasar Airport Post Office, Denpasar.

From Jimbaran the road, after crossing level country, begins to climb up onto the limestone plateau itself, and before long there is a fine view backwards over the airport and southern Bali. Immediately piles of white stone, destined for the most part for roadworks, can be seen at the side of the road. With its dry stone walls and scanty vegetation, the landscape looks like what geographers refer to as karst scenery anywhere in the world. Underground there may be secret rivers and caverns measureless to man, but here on the surface the soft dry contours present a terser, tighter-lipped picture. In place of lush rice terraces and coconut palms is a waterless landscape more reminiscent, with its chirping crickets and scent of herbs, of the south of France than the tropics.

The new red-tiled buildings you pass on the left are the new premises of the Denpasar University, **Universitas Udayana**. Two kilometers (1 1/4 miles) further on, ignore a left turn at a small junction with a statue if your destination is Ulu Watu, the road to which rises and falls, offering

---

The Balinese will flock to a major temple anywhere on the island on the occasion of its anniversary celebration (*odalan*), held every 210 days. These enthusiasts are on their way across the shallow strait to the temple on Pulau Serangan.

beautiful glimpses of the sea ahead, until finally it arrives, 21 km (14 miles) from Kuta, at its destination.

TEMPLE ABOVE THE STONE

After passing a *warung* on the right, the road swings sharply to the left and terminates in a car park where food and drink is also available. This car park serves **Pura Luhur Ulu Watu**, one of Bali's six Temples of the World and one of the finest

places on the whole island.

A wide path takes you down an incline, and then the long flight of steps of the temple itself is ahead of you. The silence, the dry, scented air and the proximity of the sea fill you with an almost unbearable expectation.

Luhur Ulu Watu probably means Above the Stone, and this is just what it is. The temple is built on a high ledge of rock extending out over the sea 76 m (250 ft) below. Nothing could be more dramatic, or more beautiful. On three sides the Indian Ocean rolls in with some

Pura Luhur, Ulu Watu. ABOVE: anything, it seems, will do as an offering; OPPOSITE: sacred monkeys?

of the biggest waves in Asia. Java is just visible straight ahead. The gods stare out in their usual sublime comprehension, but here, with all the power of nature at their feet, their serenity is doubly authentic. The white of the limestone they're carved in and the blue of the sea combine unforgettably in this pure and special place.

The temple goes back at least a thousand years and probably more. The sixteenth-century Buddhist sage Wawu Rauh is said to have achieved *moksa* (or attained Nirvana) here. Nothing could be less surprising.

Beware of Monkeys

There is only one small practical note that needs to be sounded in the general air of ecstasy and sublime transcendance. The temple is inhabited by a small band of very mischievous monkeys. They will not pause for a moment's thought before jumping down and seizing any item you leave unguarded, knowing that you will try to trick them into letting you get it back with offers of food. In the process your camera or wallet could well be dropped from one of the trees, where the monkeys usually retire, into the sea. The temple attendants say that this is a common occurrence. So be warned – but don't allow an excessive concern for your possessions to distract you from the full wonder of being where you are.

SURFING MECCA

The **Ulu Watu** that is such a special place for Bali's surfers is hardly less impressive. To get there, take the road from the car park as if you're heading to Kuta, but stop at the *warung* a couple of hundred meters down on your left. Leave any four-wheeled vehicle you may have with you in the car park – the only way down the 2 km (1 1/4 miles) to the coast is by motorbike or on foot. The path leaves the road just by the *warung*, and there are always boys there with motorbikes waiting to take you.

The way descends slowly between prickly pear cactus hedges. Shortly after the place where the bikes wait to bring people back, you go down some concrete steps into a dry valley. From here you can climb down a short bamboo ladder into the so-called cave (actually its roof has collapsed) that leads to the cove, or follow the path up to the line of *warung* and souvenir stalls that the enterprising Balinese have established on the steep sides of the slope overlooking the ocean.

out before you in all its majestic fury; away to the right Agung is outlined – on a good day – against the blue. You can sit there under the *warung*'s thatched roof and sip your iced fruit juice and watch the figures far below skimming along the great glassy slopes as if they were on skis, playing with the ocean like children in the vast lap of the gods. And as the sun goes down, straight ahead of you, it shines through the waves like light coming through the

There's not much to be seen from the little cove itself, just to the left of where the cave meets the sea. The sand is gritty and the sea bed rocky, but at least it's a place to get wet and cool off, and someone will even try to sell you a silver amulet. The really wonderful place is the highest of the *warung*.

This is perched on the edge of a ridge running up the cliff and commands a stupendous view out over the incoming surf. The spectacle is quite extraordinary. The sea is spread

green stained-glass windows of a cathedral.

Together, the temple and this surfing location make Ulu Watu among the very finest places in all Bali.

KUTA

YELLOW SANDS AND TECHNICOLOR SUNSETS

Kuta Beach extends in a long and gentle curve from just north of the airport through Kuta proper, then Legian, to the Bali Oberoi Hotel at Seminyak and beyond.

An international crowd waits for the sunset on Kuta beach, December. Sometimes the great event refuses to happen on cue, but sometimes ...

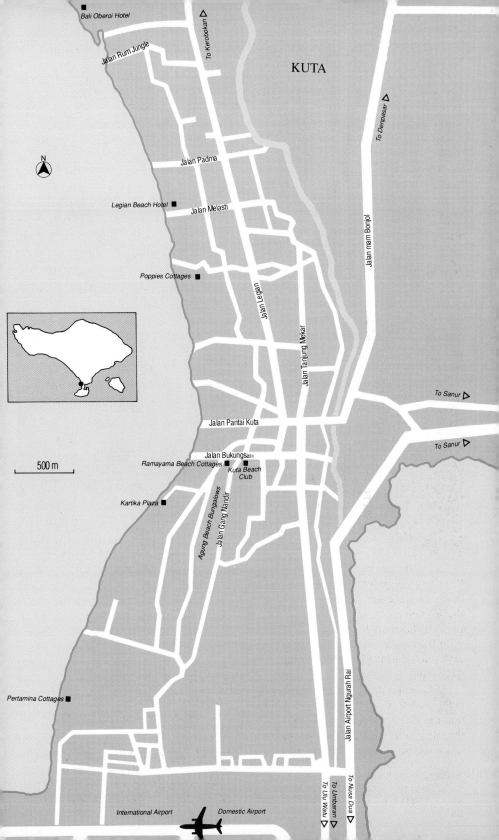

The sand is fine, hard-packed and yellow, and the surf that breaks along the length of the beach originates somewhere near the Antarctic and is famous worldwide. So too are Kuta's sunsets. It is far and away Bali's finest beach.

AN EXOTIC FAIRGROUND

Kuta is in every possible way the diametric opposite to, for instance, Nusa Dua. Its development was unplanned. It is in many places ramshackle. Very cheap food and accommodation are available everywhere. There are touts on every hand, and at the south end of the beach barely five minutes pass without someone approaching you to buy a T-shirt or give you a massage. To some people this is an intolerable intrusion, even though you do not have to walk very far in the direction

Kuta – "the circus of democratic life in the late twentieth century". ABOVE LEFT: heard melodies; ABOVE RIGHT: Balinese massage; OPPOSITE LEFT: the clothes market on Jalan Bakungsari; OPPOSITE RIGHT: hats and mats for sale.

of Legian to avoid most or all of this attention.

But the fact remains that, in addition to its supremely magnificent beach, Kuta teems with irrepressible life. The beach scene at the southern airport end resembles nothing so much as a circus, but it's the circus of democratic life in the late twentieth century and is, in many ways, something not to be missed. It's doubtful

if there's anywhere else in the world quite like it.

Australian grannies, who no doubt live very modestly back home in Adelaide, can be seen surrounded by a veritable court of hair braiders, hair beaders, massage artists, runners bearing iced beer from the beach restaurants, sellers of Dyak elixirs fresh from the jungles of Borneo – add an Italian tenor and it would be the levee scene from the opera *Der Rozenkavalier.*

Yet a few hundred meters away a hundred or more Balinese may be performing a post-cremation ceremony involving a procession in full traditional dress and the scattering of ashes on the waves accompanied by the release onto the waters of ducks, chickens and doves.

The key to it all is that while Kuta remains an extraordinarily cheap and "exotic" holiday destination for the huge numbers of Australians, Japanese, Germans, French, British and many others who flock there, this same conglomeration is an unparalleled magnet to Balinese for whom tourism represents an opportunity to make profits unheard of in other departments of the island's life. Everyone thinks he has a bargain at Kuta, and the result is a fairground of happy buying and enthusiastic selling, all under the glorious sun on one of Asia's most fabulous beaches.

The essential difference between Kuta and the more exclusive resorts to the east is that at Kuta the tourists and the local population interact by and large as in-

Kuta grew without official planning, many of the businesses in the area remain in local hands. Thus the profusion of small, budget-price *losmen* is no coincidence: they exist because Kuta grew from travelers in the sixties arriving at what was then only a medium-sized village and asking to be provided with food and a place to stay. First-class hotels have, of course, moved in since that time, and it would be a great mistake to think that Kuta only offers budget facilities. But this makes Kuta even more of a democratic phenomenon than it would otherwise have been. All tastes and all bank balances are catered for. All the world comes to Kuta Beach, and almost all Bali, it sometimes seems, is waiting there to greet them.

A DAY IN THE SUN

The day on the beach follows a regular cycle. The Surf Rescue take up their positions at 6 am and even then there are the early morning joggers and before-breakfast swimmers. By nine the beach is filling up and many of the suntan zealots are already in place. Soon the colorful scene is

dividuals. This is not to say that the one group is not very much more advantaged than the other. But whereas elsewhere most of the Balinese you will encounter will be employees of hotel syndicates, and acting out essentially the roles of servants, in Kuta the majority will be in one way or another in business on their own behalf.

This applies too, and indeed particularly, to the accommodation scene. Because

at the first of its two daily heights; the beach traders are all at work: boys with a single wood-carving wrapped in its cloth and constantly being polished, children offering to bring you ice-cold drinks for Rp200 commission, one elderly lady bearing ancient *lontar* (strips of palm leaf inscribed with sacred texts), and the inevitable and welcome sellers of hats and beach mats.

Midday sees a dramatic diminution, most of the Balinese retreating from the sun's ferocious glare and only clutches of sun-drunk northerners remaining to play frisbee relentlessly before collapsing in one of the beach bars for protracted lunches of seafood, beer and grainy Indonesian coffee to the sound of some of the older Australian and American pop hits.

If often the afternoon seems slow to take off, it's no doubt because the morning went on so long, and sunset here in the tropics is anyway very early. This, you quickly realize, is why the Indonesians get up at 4 am – in this land of eternal summer, light is gone by 5.45 in the afternoon.

THE SUNSET EVENT

Kuta's sunsets were renowned even in K'tut Tantri's day (see BIBLIOGRAPHY), and nowadays, as the coaches pull up from Nusa Dua's five-star hotels, all of Kuta, from its tattooed Japanese surfers to its Jakarta businessmen down for a week by the sea, set up their cameras where they will best catch the reflection on the wet sand, and wait.

The event itself is very like a primadonna's performance in opera – maybe the miracle will happen, maybe it won't. Sometimes Great Nature has a cough and, despite cloudless skies, the sun sinks with no more attendant glory than a fifty-cent piece dropped into a puddle. But sometimes, ah, sometimes... then the beams shoot up like chiseled shafts, the colors deepen through apricot to salmon to a final

consummating crimson, the great Indian Ocean surf laps as if entranced, and the planes drift in to land stage-right like windblown stars. And all at once it's night. The moon has established her quiet sovereignty above the palms, the motorbikes – mere spots of light – putter across the sand, plying their night trade, and the audience disperses to supper, and other pleasures and diversions.

A MEETING OF CULTURES

And on Sundays the Balinese themselves come down to savor some of the relaxing activities being enjoyed by the foreigners, those lords from other lands who are able to have what they will probably never know, holidays lasting seven days in a week. They set up goal posts on the sands or wade tentatively into the ocean still, in many cases, wearing knee-length dresses. Or else they simply gaze from above the high-water mark, in their polished Sunday shoes, at the splendor and luxury before them.

Inland, Kuta resembles a Hollywood set for a cut-price Western. A couple of paces behind the single-story facade of boutiques and restaurants is another world, one of pastoral *losmen*, coconut groves, tethered cattle and free-ranging poultry. Take your choice which is stranger – the magical world of the immemorial pastoral round or the tacked-together world of Kuta's main streets, part fashion shops, part potholes.

Stand at night at **Bemo Corner**, with your back to the beach, and the two faces of urban Kuta lie one on either hand. To your right is the **Night Market** and the cinema, each pure Indonesia. It is a world of luridly hand-painted film advertisements, flapping gaudily heroic canvases hung on scaffolding, and of interiors illuminated by kerosene lamps, hemmed in by the black and humid night. Prices are uniformly low, and the unmade-up roads dusty and uneven. The small restaurants of the Night Market have adapted themselves to the needs of the tourists, but hardly the cinema. Here seat prices are nominal, Rp250 and 350, and the seats wooden. The unmarried young stand outside or sit astride their motorbikes in the scruffy forecourt, listening to the relayed sound track. You could be anywhere in the archipelago.

But go a few hundred meters in the other direction, to the left from Bemo Corner, and there is the flashing world of the tourists' discos and bars, Peanuts, Cheaters, and the rest, and the six bars

safely at Kuta every year, but the fact remains that at certain points along the beach currents pull out seawards from the shore. Their strength varies according to the size of the surf and the phases of the moon. These danger areas are well known to the Kuta Surf Rescue teams, and every day safe-bathing areas are marked and watched all along the beach.

The problem is that the best surfing areas are exactly those areas where the currents are dangerous. Indeed, surfing is not

clustered around Peanuts that attempt to out do each other with amplified noise. Entrance tends to be free for tourists, but for Indonesians only if they can be seen to be bringing in a tourist with them. A tourist, it is assumed, can be guaranteed to pay for his entrance with drinks bought at the bar. It is astonishing so few locals complain of feeling second-rate citizens in their own land.

LETHAL RIPS

There is only one setback to Kuta Beach, but it's one that could prove very serious. Hundreds of thousands of people swim

permitted inside the designated safe-bathing areas. Experienced surfers are likely to be aware of the problem, and be able to deal with it should they begin to be pulled against their will away from shore. But even they have been known to misjudge the force of these "rips" on particular days.

The real danger lies in novices leaving the safe areas and trying their hand unsupervised in the surfing areas. The present writer did just that on his first day in Bali and was swept out way beyond the area in which the waves broke. He owes his life to

Kuta's sunset: "the great Indian Ocean surf laps as if entranced" – and some people are reluctant to call it a day.

the prompt intervention of the Surf Rescue, who noticed him even though he was far from the flagged area they are watching.

A book containing the names of those rescued can be inspected at the Badung Tourist Office in Denpasar.

The **Kuta Surf Rescue** service is run by the Badung Government Tourist Office in Denpasar. It maintains four stations along the beach, at Kuta, Half-Legian, Legian and at the Kuta Palace Hotel. In addition, the Bali Oberoi pays for a private service. Officially known as the Badung Surf Life Saving Bali, the service was set up in 1972 in response to the increased use of Kuta Beach for surfing and the number of lives being lost there.

There are 23 men employed by the service, five captains (earning Rp3,250 a day), five No 2s (earning Rp3,090) and 13 rescuers (earning Rp2,590). They are on duty every day of the year, with the one exception of the Balinese New Year, Nyepi, when no one is allowed on the beach anyway. Their hours are 6 am to 6 pm.

The service operates with additional help from their counterparts at Cottesloe Beach, Perth, Western Australia from whom advice and materials have come over the years.

Remember – if you are in danger, try not to panic and raise one hand high above your head. This is the international distress signal and is what the Surf Rescue are looking for. If you do swim, swim sideways, out of the current, not against it.

KUTA'S HISTORY

It was probably here that Gajah Mada invaded from Java in the fourteenth century with his Majapahit forces. In 1580 the Englishman Sir Francis Drake may have called in for provisions. In 1597 a small Dutch expedition of three ships under Cornelius de Houtman dropped anchor off Kuta and a party was landed. Later, the ships sailed round to the better anchorage off Padangbai, with the added purpose of being near the court of the Dewa Agung, the most powerful of Bali's chiefs, and his court at Gelgel, near Klungkung.

In the succeeding centuries Bali became a source of slaves, sold to Java but also as far afield as Mauritius. Kuta (encompassing also the anchorages nearby on the east coast) was the center for that trade.

But Kuta had always been to some extent disreputable, an area where vagabonds congregated and foreigners were allowed to settle. Parallels with its modern character needn't be emphasized.

WHERE TO STAY

There is so much accommodation Kuta and Legian it is only feasible to mention some of the less inexpensive places that intending visitors might want to contact to make advance reservations. The small *losmen* which are a specialty of the resort can only really be selected after inspection on the ground.

Beginning in the south, **Pertamina Cottages** (© 51161; 178 rooms; rates: expensive) was constructed initially for the benefit of executives of the Indonesian state oil company, whose name it still bears, but financial problems in the industry necessitated its being sold off and now it functions as one of the country's better hotels. Heads of state have stayed here for international conferences, and Gough Whitlam once wrote in its VIP visitors' book: "If there be a Paradise on Earth, this is it." It may be very close to the airport and suffering from an eroding coastline, but otherwise everything, but everything, is provided.

Balinese life is by no means all temple ritual: TOP: a seller of very untraditional masks, Denpasar; BELOW: massage on Kuta beach. Note the numbered sun hats – all masseurs have to obtain a licence. Half an hours's massage will cost something under one US dollar.

The **Kartika Plaza** (© 51067-9; 120 rooms; rates: average and above) is also sited on the sea, though the beach is not at its best until a little further north. The hotel boasts a Korean restaurant.

Once you arrive at Jalan Bakungsari, running at right angles to the sea and joining the beach at a large cheap clothes market, you are in the thick of things. Progressing inland, and all on the right of the road, you have **Agung Beach Bungalows** (© 51263/4; 70 rooms; rates: moderate), the **Kuta Beach Club** (© 51-261/2; 96 rooms; rates: average and above) and the **Ramayana Seaside Cottages** (© 51864-6; rates: moderate). All have bungalow-style rooms and are within three minutes' walk of the beach.

Particularly good value is the **Kuta Village Inn** (© 51059; rates: moderate), tucked away down a narrow lane, or *gang*, a little further along the road on the same side. The welcome is very friendly, and special arrangements can often be made after discussion with the management. There is a choice of rooms, some air-conditioned, some with ceiling fan, and prices vary accordingly.

On the next road north, Jalan Pantal Kuta, stands the **Kuta Beach Hotel** (© 51361; 32 rooms; rates: average and above), two hundred meters south of the site of the hotel with the same name that was Kuta's first hostelry back in the thirties. There's a Garuda office in the lobby, and Japanese dishes in the restaurant. Also on the same street is the very reasonable **Ida Beach Inn Bungalows** (© 51205 and 51934; 4l rooms; rates: moderate, with no service charges added).

Tucked away along Poppies Lane and just past the restaurant are the cottages of the same name, **Poppies Cottages** (© 51059 and 51149; 20 rooms; rates: moderate). This famous and very popular place has thatched bungalow rooms in a garden setting on the standard Kuta, indeed Balinese, pattern. Self-catering facilities, and baby-sitters, can be made available.

One of many places on the main Jalan Legian is **Fourteen Roses** (© 51156 and 51835; rates: average and above). There is a swimming pool, but no restaurant.

Back on the beach itself, and still continuing north, there is the **Legian Beach Hotel** (© 51711; 110 rooms; rates: average and above). This stands at the end of the road at right angles to the beach known as Jalan Melasti. Parallel to this, and the next lane north, is Jalan Padma, where the **Bali Mandira Cottages** (© 51381; 96 rooms; rates: average and above) are located.

North again, and again right on the beach, is the **Kuta Palace Hotel** (© 51461/2 and 51879; 100 rooms; rates: average and above) while last of all, 6 km (10 miles) north of the airport, is the **Bali Oberoi** (© 51061; 75 rooms; rates: expensive). More expensive than anywhere at Nusa Dua, the Bali Oberoi was, like Pertamina Cottages, built as an executive haven. It is one of the truly special places to stay in Bali – private, intimate and well-managed. It was not always grand, however; in the years immediately prior to 1978 it was semi-derelict and a hippie haven of international standing. Life there now is probably a good deal less exciting, but immeasurably more discreet.

Kuta is famous for its inexpensive accommodation, and it really is possible to stay within minutes of this incomparably fine beach for something in the region of US$2.00 a day. The best *losmen* consist of the simplest possible rooms set around a lush Balinese garden, probably with a shrine in the middle. Inspecting them is half the pleasure, though it's always hard telling the owner that you've decided to stay somewhere else. Nevertheless, you'll need somewhere to stay that first day while you look around, and you could do a lot worse than opt for the **Puspa Beach Inn** (© 51988; 8 rooms; rates: inexpensive) a few meters down a *gang* off Bakungsari Street. As at most *losmen*, breakfast is included in the absurdly low price.

WHERE TO EAT

The restaurants in Kuta are as varied as the accommodation. Prices, however, tend to be competitive, with the more expensive places confined to the classier hotels. The variety in Kuta's eateries lies not in their prices but in their cuisines.

You can eat Japanese, Mexican, German, Chinese – the only problem is actually getting Balinese food, but even that is possible.

Service charges are not a feature of Kuta's restaurants. Only Poppies even mentions them, going on to say that they are "included." Likewise, tipping is not really expected.

Once you've been to **Made's Warung** on Jalan Pantai Kuta you may well decide you never want to try anywhere else. The range of food is vast, from strawberries to roast beef and encompassing Indonesian and Chinese specialties on the way. The menu overflows onto the very walls, and the atmosphere is half Paris and half Amsterdam. It is at one and the same time *the* fashionable meeting-place and a very congenial hidey-hole at any time of day. It's both shabby and chic, and one of its great virtues is that, in contrast to most other places, there is for much of the time no music. A couple of glasses of *arak madu* (palm spirit with orange juice and honey) have seen many a lunch extended into the mid-afternoon, with the patrons finally managing to stumble the short distance along the road and collapse on the beach just in time for the sunset.

Poppies on Poppies Lane is an old favorite now become chic; but the food remains excellent, and the restaurant is so popular that tourists come there from Sanur and Nusa Dua and it is advisable to book during July and August.

For some mysterious reason, there are three Mexican restaurants in Kuta/Legian. **TJ's**, down Poppies Lane, is very fine, with giant bamboo settees for pre-dinner drinks and appetizers. In addition to the usual fare – *tacos, tostadas, enchiladas,*

etc. – there are excellent salads and, yes, roast potatoes. Fine food in well-designed and comfortable surroundings.

La Barong, opposite Made's Warung, and the **Legian Roxi**, up Jalan Legian on the right, just past Jalan Padma, offer equally fiery specialties, the latter with pizza and spaghetti, "freezing cold beer" and videos also on tap in the heartier Kuta style.

Many establishments go for this vigorous ambiance – **Glory** on Legian Road,

nearly opposite the Legian Roxi, for example, with its Outback Brekkies, 1.6 liter jugs of Harvey Wallbanger and "Satisfaction or No Charge" guarantees. A Balinese "as much as you can eat for Rp2000" Sunday lunch seems the sort of thing you could only dream about after all those Wallbangers.

The **Bali Indah Seafood** restaurant, opposite the Casablanca bar on Jalan Bunisari, offers excellent Chinese food in down-to-earth surroundings. The spicy Sichuan dishes are especially fine.

Northerners who long for potatoes and home-made sausages will find the land of their heart's desire at the **Swiss Restaurant** (© 51735), on the right just before Jalan Melasti on Jalan Legian. *Bratwurst,*

The best eating in Kuta combines quality with informality, amiability with economy, and all under a traditional Balinese roof. The variety of cuisines is enormous, and the relaxed joviality of many establishments is a joy.

wiener kartoffelsalat and *apfelstrudel* rub shoulders with *fondue bourguignonne* and the Balinese buffets on Thursdays and Saturdays. The Swiss and West German consular representatives understandably operate from this address.

The very reasonable **Daruma Japanese Restaurant** (℃ 23906), close to Bemo Corner and almost opposite Made's Warung, proves that, in Bali at least, Japanese food can be both filling and need not break the bank.

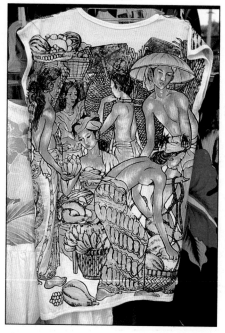

Double Six may be a little hard to find but its style and live entertainment make the effort worthwhile. Take the lane known as Jalan Enam-Enam (which means Six Six anyway), the second lane running from Jalan Legian to the sea north of Jalan Padma. The menu features Italian pastas with seafood and good salads as well. On nights when there is a show, a special buffet dinner is laid out.

Wayan's Tavern (℃ 51578) on Jalan Bunisari offers genuine espresso coffee, while **Dayu 1** (℃ 51498), round the corner on Jalan Bakungsari, offers breakfasts at any time of day and inexpensive, wholesome food prepared in a clean and visible kitchen.

The Green House (℃ 51193) on Jalan Pantai Kuta offers Chinese and European dishes, plus Balinese dance shows. Free transport is available from hotels in the Kuta and Legian areas, as it is to **Paul Nyoman's Bar and Restaurant/Pizzeria** on Jalan Legian, where the food is served in a luxuriant garden setting.

If you want to eat with your toes actually in the sand, then head for the **Batu Karang Beach Bar and Restaurant**. And lastly, for very cheap but often excellent food, try **Depot Kuta** (℃ 51155) in Kuta's Night Market. There are several very inexpensive restaurants and food stalls here, but this one, specializing in Chinese food, is among the best.

DISCO FEVER

Kuta's nightlife is both raucous and extensive. buses of pub crawlers in full voice bump down Jalan Bakungsari on set nights of the week (well advertised in leaflets handed out on the beach), and certain discos cooperate to ensure there's a party every night of the week.

At **Casablanca** on Jalan Bunisari the entertainment begins early and consists of drinking competitions interspersed with rock 'n' roll videos. Six minutes' walk along Jalan Legian, on the left, is the **SC Club**, where a giant video screen has enabled them to do away with the drinking competitions. Both of these bars tend to be busiest before the discos get under way at about 11:30 pm.

The two main discos in Kuta itself are within a few meters of each other – **Peanuts** ("T-shirts, singlets, shorts, thongs, BLOODY WELCOME MATE!") and **Cheaters** (℃ 51638). Both are large with big dance floors and a discriminatory policy toward locals (see p.129). Not far away is **Rivoli** ("for serious nightlifers") with live bands "direct from overseas."

Rather more exclusive, and operating fixed-entrance charges, are **Chez Gado Gado**, on the sea some way north of

Legian, and **Double Six**. See the section on Kuta's restaurants above for instructions on how to get to Double Six; to get to Gado Gado you really need to charter a bemo as it's several kilometers and at the end of a long, rather rough lane.

At the time of writing Gado Gado was running "party nights" on Tuesdays, Thursdays and Saturdays and Double Six on Mondays and Fridays. Sunday belongs to **Bruna's**, on the beachfront at Kuta.

Local regulations stop the discos at

SHOPPING

Kuta is an excellent place for shopping, combining, in the best places, quality and cheapness. There are some good clothes shops on Jalan Bunisari, and some beautiful shirts and T-shirts can be seen at **Mr T-shirt** on Jalan Pantai Kuta. Artistic and original designs are on sale at **Ari's Hair and Beauty House** – turn left at the end of Jalan Bakungsari before it enters

2:30 am but a different set of rules applies to a group of bars midway between Kuta and Legian. When the parties are over, people tend to go to either **Il Pirata** for cappuccino and pizza, or **Yani's** for still more drinks.

One last alternative deserves mention. In the small laneway beside Made's Warung is the **Tuak Bar**, a covered area of concrete and wooden benches where the alcoholic juice of the palm tree is served out of plastic buckets into various sized bamboo cups. Entertainment is provided by anyone who has a guitar or harmonica and the place closes when the *tuak* runs out.

the clothes market next to the beach, and the shop is the first you come to on the right.

Batik can be found everywhere, but the muted colors of "old" batik are particularly attractive and are available at the **Taruko Shop**, some way down Jalan Legian, in Legian itself, on the right.

Very cheap cassettes are so much a feature of Kuta that there are over a dozen shops selling nothing else. Doubts about

Every Balinese is an artist, or so the early visitors to the island claimed. Perhaps the truth is that all people everywhere are. OPPOSITE: a hand-painted T-shirt; ABOVE: work is displayed and admired in a fashionable boutique in Kuta.

quality can apparently be allayed by choosing ones recorded in Jakarta rather than in Bali itself. Advice, and a very wide selection of titles, can be had at **Kul-Kul** on Jalan Bakungsari. Many people spend hours out of the sun listening to music in such places, and if you stay long enough you'll be provided with free soft drinks into the bargain.

There are several bookshops specializing in holiday reading. Particularly recommended, both for the range and quality of its stock, is the **Kertai Bookshop** on Jalan Pantai Kuta, on the left as you walk toward the beach. New and secondhand books are available and can be traded in at half price when you've finished with them.

For antiques, **East West** and **Auang's** each offer a wide selection, including gold and silver jewelry.

There are many paintings on sale in Kuta, but it's far better to buy such things not here but a mere hour's drive away, in Ubud.

SOUTH BALI: TANAH LOT TO UBUD

This area of Bali in many ways contains the island's essence. Here is the intense rice cultivation on the banks of the fast-flowing rivers that rush down from the mountains, cutting themselves earthy gorges as they do so and providing for the irrigation that has always been the basis of the island's prosperity. This abundant water supply, and the immensely fertile volcanic soils that it feeds, is the key to Bali's ceaseless rice production, which continues regardless of season, so that the rainy season is as much an inconvenience as a blessing. The great lakes in the volcanic calderas ensure an endless supply, and this in turn guarantees food production.

Famine, so common elsewhere in Asia, is in Bali only the product of political upheaval or volcanic eruption. Thanks to the

relatively new "miracle" rice, three crops a year are now normal, and all stages of growth can often be seen in adjacent fields, providing the different tones of yellow and green that have so delighted painters.

And, of course, it is this agricultural abundance that has allowed Bali to develop its arts. Leisure time has never been in short supply, and with carving, painting and metalwork all originally dedicated to a religion that looked up to the hills from where the abundance came, it can seem as if the whole formed a self-contained, beautiful and life-enhancing system. And so many of the island's first visitors saw it.

The area of which Ubud is generally considered the center is the heart of all this. East Bali is lush too, but the plains are less extensive, there are many subsidiary ridges of hills, and the region is subject too to earthquakes. North Bali is a mere coastal strip. Bali south of Denpasar, now so prosperous on account of tourism, was not so long ago seen as a more or less arid waste. And West Bali has always been considered a rocky, waterless and infertile wilderness.

For the purposes of this guide, the central southern area will be considered as running from Tanah Lot in the west to Bangli in the east, with Ubud as its center.

TANAH LOT

This celebrated but overrated site consists of a small temple perched on a rocky islet some one hundred meters out from the coast. Except at high tide you can walk across over the rocks, but you will not be allowed up into the temple – it's locked except at festival times. But most people have little desire to go there; what they

Tanah Lot, attractively seen in near-monochrome. The coach-loads of photographers arriving to catch the temple outlined against the sunset have rendered that particular image one of modern Asia's banalities.

want to do is photograph it from the shore, preferably against the backdrop of a sunset.

There are essentially three places from which this picturesque if slightly twee ensemble can be captured on film: from down in the cove itself, from along the low cliff where the row of small restaurants is situated, and from the headland on the right. From this last position a natural arch in the rocks to the north can also be taken, with Mount Batur in the background.

A Holy Snake

Tanah Lot has little to keep you for more than a very brief visit. You can, while down in the cove, see the supposedly "holy snake" or guardian of the temple, which lies conveniently coiled on a ledge in a small cave. Boys will illuminate it for you with a small flashlight and collect a donation for the service.

The temple itself has five small thatched shrines and is thought to date from the sixteenth century when the priest Danghyang Nirartha crossed over to Bali from Java floating on a leaf. He instructed several temples to be built, and Tanah Lot is said to be one of these, as is the far more spectacular temple at Ulu Watu.

Entrance to the beach area adjacent to the temple is Rp200. You will be asked to pay an additional donation but there's no need to do so.

Tanah Lot is 12 km (7 1/2 miles) from Kediri on the main road from Denpasar to Tabanan. Kediri is 5 km (3 1/8 miles) beyond **Kapal**, the village where carved architectural details are produced, seemingly for the whole of Bali.

It's easy to get to Tanah Lot by bemo, though most people arrive on organized tours. Bemo rates are: Denpasar (Ubung) to Kediri, Rp450; Kediri to Tanah Lot, Rp300.

Taman Ayun, Mengwi. The temple is especially spacious and, surrounded as it is by a wide moat, the sense of peace is remarkable. One of the temple's multi-tiered black *meru* can just be seen in the center of the photograph.

MENGWI

Taman Ayun, the Water Temple at Mengwi, is a very attractive, peaceful place. Built on rising grass slopes and partly surrounded by a wide moat, it is spacious and almost trim in a way that is not very characteristic of Balinese temples. As if to establish this garden-like quality, there is a pool with a fountain in it on the left as you enter the first compound.

In the second compound, in the bottom left-hand corner, is a small tower that can be climbed; the top provides a good viewpoint for photos of the temple and its watery surrounds. Immediately below, gnarled frangipani trees exhibit their fabulous blossoms.

The last, or inner, court contains ten very fine *meru*, the tall tiered towers thatched in black *ijuk*, a fiber derived from the sago palm. The number of tiers is always uneven, as with the tiers on cremation towers. Here the tallest have 11.

The inner court also contains a fine stone *padmasana*, in effect a giant and highly ornate chair on which it is hoped the unseen supreme god will deign to sit on days of high festival. The back of the chair is oriented toward Agung. Also notable is an ornate brick and stone shrine with a thatched roof on the left. At the corner of each base is a carving of Garuda attacking Naga. The entire inner court is surrounded by a miniature walled moat that echoes the great moat that nearly encircles the temple as a whole.

To the left of the upper part of Taman Ayun is a lush, overgrown area, abandoned to nature and silent except for the chirping of insects. It's a place for the poetic moment, and for thoughts such as that somewhere, somehow it may be possible to be happy. With its spaciousness and lily-covered waters, Taman Ayun is itself naturally host to such thoughts.

More mundanely, on the far side of the outer moat overlooking the temple, there

is the **Water Garden Restaurant** (rates: moderate) where straightforward Indonesian and Chinese dishes are available. Its real attraction is its location. It boasts two telephone numbers – 4318 and 6863 – but these are in fact both for the "head office" in Denpasar.

SANGEH

An exceptionally pleasant winding country road links Mengwi and the Monkey Forest at Sangeh, 9 km (5 5/8 miles) away. Take the road on which the Water Temple stands, turning left as you leave the precinct. Turn left after approximately 5 km (3 1/8 miles), then left again after a further 2 km (1 1/4 miles). The forest is then on your left, opposite a car park.

Sangeh consists of some 10 hectares (24 acres) of *pala* trees in the middle of which is a temple. It is in fact a sacred wood. About a thousand monkeys are said to inhabit the area, and they too are "sacred."

There are stories of coach loads of tourists overwhelming Sangeh from morning till night, a horror only exceeded by the bands of thieving monkeys that leap on you at the least rustle of a packet of peanuts. A visit at about 4 pm, however, makes it possible to appreciate the real beauty of the place.

The trees are tall and symmetrical, some reaching to a height of 50 m (164 ft) with no side branches. The place is scented by the five-petaled flowers of the trees which lie scattered underfoot. The shady cool and the silence induce an air of sanctity, and the temple is simple and potent. It is dedicated to Vishnu and much visited by farmers.

Monkey Kings

There are around a thousand monkeys, organized in two groups, east and west, each with its king. No monkey will cross into the other group's territory. At sunset, they retreat up to the tops of the trees to sleep.

Locals will tell you the biggest monkeys are "of course" the kings (thereby providing an insight into Indonesian attitudes to politics). They also insist no dead body of an old monkey as opposed to younger ones killed accidentally has even been found.

Entrance to Sangeh is by donation (Rp200). Young men will attach themselves to you and chat as you walk along, but by the time you are ready to leave you will realize you have in fact made use of the services of a guide, and a payment will be expected.

The statue at the entrance is of Hanuman, the white monkey god of the *Ramayana* stories and the *kecak* dance.

UBUD

Ubud itself doesn't have the feeling of a town – more an extended village. Its long main street, running east to west, is on the main road to nowhere, and a relaxed, yet never lethargic, ambiance pervades the place.

There are many tourists at Ubud as it's the main attraction for the sizable minority who come to Bali for art rather than for sun, sea and surf. This influx of foreigners has proved a problem in the past, but some sort of an accommodation now seems to have been reached and there are no obvious signs of local resentment. No doubt Ubud's obvious prosperity is a main part of the reason.

Ubud is the best place in Bali to see dance dramas and to buy paintings, and one of the better places to enjoy the relaxing effects of watching other people at work in the countryside.

Legong Dance

One feature of about Ubud is that they do things in style there. You know from the very first strike on the gong that the performance culminating in the *legong* dance (every Monday at the Puri or Palace) is the real thing. The concentration of the *gamelan* as they play their introductory overture, their costumes and the beautifully painted mounts for their instruments, the setting itself – all are perfect. It's an introduction, and you settle down for the extended pleasure confident that nothing is going to be stinted. And the relish with which, later in the week, the narrator begins his story in the *wayang kulit* puppet theater is almost as reassuring.

Yet all these accomplished performers are in the daytime ordinary workers in res-

Lotus Cafe, on the other side. Full details of drama performances, plus tickets, are available here.

Where to Stay

There is a vast amount of accommodation available in Ubud and you can pay anything from US$1 to US$60 for it. The following is a selection.

Beginning from the Campuhan end, the area down by the two bridges and Murni's Warung, there is the **Hotel Tjam-**

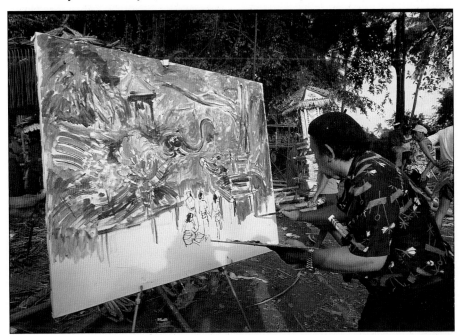

taurants, shops or in the fields. These are genuine folk dramas, like the European medieval morality plays – you see the Monkey King or Shiva, but really it's the local butcher or candlestick maker. What is all this sophisticated talk, you wonder, about professionalism?

Information

Bemos from Denpasar to Ubud leave from the Kereneng terminus; the fare is Rp500.

Ubud has a market every third day, from 5 am to 3 pm.

There is a particularly helpful Tourist Office on the main street not far from the

puhan (ie. Campuhan in unreformed spelling; (© 28871; rates: average and above). This is a long-established bungalow hotel on the steep-sloping bank of the river. A path zigzags down and there are bungalows dotted around in twos at various levels. It has a tennis court and swimming pool; Walter Spies, the artist, once lived there. It's upmarket but not new; however, the resulting ambiance might suit some tastes. There are

Painting from life like this is not at all typical of Balinese practice. But Bali is increasingly coming under the influence of foreign customs, and the Balinese are showing themselves remarkably able to adapt while remaining, in other ways, exactly the same.

phones by the beds, and the royal suite actually runs to a hot bath! The feeling is undeniable, though, that this was once a somewhat better place than it is now.

Up the hill from here, on the other side of the road, are the **Munut Bungalows** (rates: moderate). This is actually three separate establishments, two of them perched on bluffs above the road (and possibly, therefore, slightly noisy). The third, set back a little among the rice paddies, is superb and the nicest place I saw in Ubud.

Paintings by the owner are everywhere and there is a *gamelan* set out and ready for action. Little bridges cross lily ponds. This delightful retreat is directly opposite **Ardjuna's Inn** (© 22809; rates: inexpensive), an unassuming *losmen* with simple, clean rooms. It's next door to the top entrance to Antonio Blanco's House (see p.144).

In the center of Ubud, close to the *puri* and the intersection with the Monkey Forest Road is **Hans Snel's Siti Bungalows** (© 28690; rates: average and above). A short way down a lane, this is classy, even smart, accommodation adjacent to the restaurant and cocktail bar of the same name. It may seem just a little too discreet for some, and there is no hot water on tap (though this is not something many visitors feel the need for in this climate). Back on the road, the **Puri Saraswati** (rates: moderate) offers standard bungalow rooms around a courtyard. And down the Monkey Forest Road, on the left,

Tjanderi's (or Candri's; rates: inexpensive) is a long-established, popular staging post for overlanders.

To find the small, friendly and very inexpensive **Rama Sita Pension**, turn down the lane that leaves the main road immediately next to the Nomad Cafe and follow it till it dips down and forms a T-junction with another road – the pension is ahead of you. For the very quiet **Jati Homestay** (rates: moderate), follow the road known as Padang Tegal and it's some way down on the right. Lastly, **Sudharsana's Bungalows**, (rates: inexpensive), on the main street offers good value for money with straightforward accommodation.

People also, of course, come to Ubud, get to know artists, find places to stay far from the tourist trails, and live on for months virtually as part of the family. To find such places takes time, though, and to list them in a book like this would be an unwarranted intrusion.

Where to Eat

Easily the nicest place to eat in Ubud is the **Cafe Lotus** (rates: average and above). It is almost opposite the Tourist Office, and both food and ambiance are superb. Hundreds of pink lilies stretch their necks like flamingos in the pond, and music chosen with discretion (no Vivaldi's "Four Seasons" here) plays unobtrusively as the first Gin Fizz arrives. The menu the day I ate there offered (among many other delights) real wheat bread – not so easy to come by in Bali – salads with olive oil dressing, freshly made pasta with mushrooms, and strawberry tart.

Every stomach now and again insists on something it knows and preferably loves. The Lotus Cafe unashamedly provides for these moments, and the quality is outstanding. The pleasure of eating delicacies you long for but never expect to meet on this side of the world is compounded by paying a third or even a quarter of what you would pay for them in Paris, Frankfurt or Los Angeles.

The Lotus Cafe is open from 11 am to 9 pm, and closed on Mondays.

Murni's Warung (rates: moderate), down by the old suspension and modern road bridges over the river, is also a fashionable place. It too specializes in Western food – head here for unexpected items such as muesli, bacon, corned beef and *guacamole*. It also stocks souvenirs, books on Bali, and some secondhand novels (but see the next entry for a better selection). Murni's is open from 8 am to 8 pm (hence it's a good place for breakfast) and closed on Wednesdays and selected holidays.

At the **Menara Restaurant** (rates: inexpensive), on the main street near the Tourist Office, they don't have much idea how to prepare Western food but the ambiance can be delightful if, on a sunny morning, you happen to drop in for breakfast when the schoolchildren are rehearsing their *gamelan* and dance routines on a stage that is part of the restaurant. Most notable, though, is the lending library run by the proprietor – this has a very wide selection of books of all kinds in several languages. You pay Rp2,000 deposit and then Rp200 per volume. It provides a service unparalleled in Ubud.

The **Nomad Wine Bar and Restaurant** (rates: moderate), further down the main street in the direction of Denpasar, is a very pleasant place, open from 8 am to 10 pm. There's live music at night and a relaxed ambiance prevails. The owner also offers a guide service with car.

Puri's Snackbar on the other side of the road (rates: inexpensive) achieves the impossible by combining quality and sophistication with very low prices. Open 7 am till midnight, it is the latest place to close in Ubud.

Further toward Denpasar, the **Raya Coffee House** (rates: moderate) is congenial, while close to the Jati Homestay the **Jati Restaurant** (rates: moderate) offers good Indonesian food and some Balinese specialties.

Eating cheaply is no problem in Ubud. Many of the *losmen* down the Monkey Forest Road have small restaurants attached where you can eat well for under US$2. Again, Tjanderi's (Candri's) can be recommended.

Museums

There are two important museums exhibiting Balinese paintings in Ubud. The more recently established (1982) **Museum Neka** has 13 rooms and orders its material

into styles. This, therefore, is the place to go if Balinese art seems to you either all the same or a confusion of contrasting tendencies. The museum is about 1 km (5/8 mile) beyond the bridge by Murni's Warung; carry straight on up the road on the other side of the river and it's on your right. Opening hours: 8 am to 4 pm; entrance fee: Rp200.

The older **Puri Lukisan Museum** (founded in 1954) is in the center of the village and contains ten rooms – seven in the main building and three in a separate gallery on the left as you arrive. Again, all styles of Balinese art are on show, though less clearly categorized than at the Neka. Nevertheless, many paintings crucial to the history of Balinese art and the changes brought about by the arrival of artists from

Ubud. OPPOSITE: the lotuses that give their name to the village's most delectable eating place; ABOVE: deer-like Balinese cattle being taken for a walk.

Europe between the wars can be seen here. Times and fee as for the Neka.

More useful still, however, is the display in a separate building a short walk across a paddy field away (follow a sign labeled "Exhibition" pointing right as you come out of the main museum). Here there are a large number of pictures for sale. As they are by a wide variety of artists, and as they have fixed prices marked on the back of their labels, a wander around here can give you a very fair idea of the going rate for Balinese art, and the kind of prices you might consider reasonable should you want to negotiate with the local painters themselves in their private galleries elsewhere in the district.

An Artist's House

If museums tend to make you cross-eyed with their bewildering variety, somewhere that is all of a piece and a work of art in its own right is **Antonio Blanco's House**. Erotic illuminated poems hang beside fantasy portraits of the very lady who will probably let you in and politely take the Rp200 entrance fee, the painter's Balinese wife. You are unlikely to get to meet the venerable Filipino artist himself, but you can certainly look around his studio and gain a real sense of what Ubud and Bali once were, both for him and for the other expatriate artists who made it their home.

A Dog Orchestra

Ubud evenings are exceptionally pleasant. There are performances somewhere or other every night, and as likely as not old Gusti Moleh will sell you a ticket as you wander along the main street at dusk. His *Sita Leaps into the Fire* appears in the lavishly produced volume *Paintings from the Collection of Dr Sukarno* (Peking, 1956) and he will without doubt invite

Women returning from the fields near Ubud. The central area of Bali is the island's heartland, a rich alluvial rice-growing region where the many ancient monuments testify to a long history of human settlement and sophistication.

you to inspect his very well-worn copy of the volume. Ubud is altogether a genial and friendly place, and if you stay at all long you'll quickly get to know a number of the local artists and characters.

Sometimes it's necessary to travel the 13 km (8 1/8 miles) to Bona to see some of the dance dramas (see p.64), but transport from Ubud always goes with the ticket. By the time you get back, Ubud's dogs will be getting ready for their night's performance.

They come into their own after about 10 pm. One begins to howl and they all pitch in until it sounds like a rehearsal for the All-Ubud Dog Orchestra. They are very much their own masters – neither wild nor tame, neither loved nor wholly rejected, neither individuals nor exactly a pack, neither habitually aggressive nor particularly friendly. They are the Dogs of Ubud. Before long, they'll constitute a tourist attraction in themselves.

Ubud on Foot

There are some good walks around Ubud and the best way to find your way around them is to acquire the amusing little publication entitled *Bali Path Finder*, a skittishly annotated map featuring Bali as a whole on the one side of the sheet, and Ubud and environs on the other (obainable from many outlets in the village).

The sites covered in ROUND CENTRAL BALI (below) are all slightly or considerably too far from Ubud itself to be reached on foot. It is possible to rent push-bikes (average rate: Rp1500 per day) but the countryside around Ubud is far from flat. Better to rely on the bemos, or rent motorized transport, with or without a driver.

SAYAN

To find Sayan, follow the road across the bridges until, after about 5 km (3 1/8 miles) you meet a left, signposted to

Denpasar. Take this road for 3 km (1 1/8 miles) or so, watching out for a sign on the right to **Sayan Terrace Cottages** (rates: moderate). A short walk will take you to this spectacularly sited accommodation, perched on the edge of a very beautiful view. It's like a scene from any of a thousand Ubud paintings – terraces descending steeply to the Ayung River far below, people at work in the rice fields, green areas of forest modulating into blue as the eye rises to focus, on a good day, on

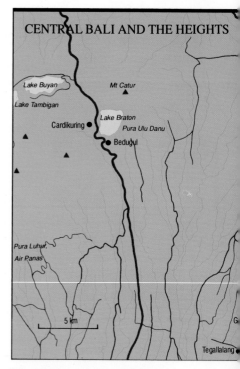

CENTRAL BALI AND THE HEIGHTS

Mount Abang in the distance.

The proprietor is himself, unsurprisingly, a painter, and his pictures are for sale at the small *warung* on the road.

ROUND CENTRAL BALI

The area to the east of Ubud is crowded with sites of antiquarian interest. The following pages describe the most interesting of these in the form of a round tour, but it should be noted that to do justice to all these places in the same day would be, in the Balinese climate, a near impossibility.

Leaving Ubud by way of the main street in the general direction of Denpasar, turn left at the first junction, where all the Denpasar-bound traffic turns right. This road will take you to Pujung (15 km or 9 3/8 miles away). This is a most attractive road, scenic in a very Balinese way, seemingly unfrequented, yet brimming with artists' workplaces and sales stalls.

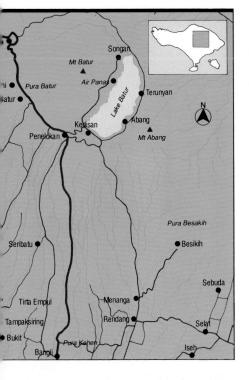

TEGALALANG

Banana-tree Carvings

On the way, you will pass through Tegalalang, a small center for the production of painted, softwood statues, usually of fruit or plants. As you drive up the road you pass small shops, each specializing in one particular form or style. When you finally reach Pujung you are in a place where, it is said, the main occupation of the populace is the manufacture of the banana-tree carvings

to be seen at tourist centers all over the island.

Turn right at Pujung and descend to the bottom of the valley where, at **Sebatu**, there are some attractive public baths. From there the road climbs again, past many shops offering painted softwood carvings of all kinds, to the road junction where you bear left for, after 1 km (5/8 mile), Tampaksiring.

TIRTA EMPUL

The **Sukarno Palace** at Tampaksiring is reached up a good number of steps – it is a fifties period pile with Western carpets, Western windows and international-level security. It is built in two sections connected by a footbridge over a small valley.

At the foot of the steps is the important site of **Tirta Empul**, consisting of holy springs, public baths and a temple. The water emerges from the rock into a large basin, and from there into the bathing pool. The water is considered both sacred and magical, so bathing in it is a very popular pursuit. The actual temple is one of the six most important in Bali and creates an unusually vivid impression – it's recently been restored.

GUNUNG KAWI

Take the road south from Tampaksiring in the direction of Gianyar and you will shortly be at the site of the King's Tombs, or Gunung Kawi, on the left of the road.

A few meters from the car park, steps begin to descend the side of the steep valley. If you arrive at the end of a long day or, worse still, in the heat of the early afternoon, you might be content to regard the site from above – in this case, go down a few dozen steps from the car park to where there is a convenient viewing point. If you opt to inspect the whole thing at close quarters, descend until the path crosses the River Pakrisan by a bridge and young boys far below have set up a lucrative business diving for coins thrown from the parapet above.

The remains consist of large mausoleums, formal rectangular shapes cut into the rock and without ornamental design. There are four on your left before you cross the bridge, five ahead of you on the other side, and one last one further down the valley. There are also passages cut into the rock, rather reminiscent of war time pillboxes.

The whole feeling is almost Egyptian in its formality. The monuments are thought to date from the eleventh century and to be the resting place for the ashes, or the actual bodies, of King Anak Wungsu, who reigned over Bali from AD1049 to 1077, and his wives and sons.

THE MOON OF PEJENG

Continuing south, after another 11 km (6 1/4 miles) you reach Pejeng and, on the left of the road, **Pura Panataram Sasih**. This temple, though another of the Balinese top six, is largely famous for its gigantic bronze drum, known as the Moon Face. It is more than two meters long, its striking end 1.6 meters in diameter, and it is a thousand years old, dating from the ninth century. Unfortunately, it is kept high up under a roof and consequently is not very clearly visible.

One kilometer further on, on your right, is the **Pura Kebo Edan**, or Crazy Buffalo Temple, best known for its statue of the dancing Bhima, strongman from the epic poem the *Mahabharata*, with its multiple penises.

Only a short distance further, on the other side of the road, is the **Archaeological Museum** (Museum Arkeologi) containing a variety of historical objects and fossils.

YEH PULU

Shortly after this, the road divides, turning right for Ubud and left for Gianyar. There is, however, also another, untarred road

that leads off from this junction – follow this for 2 km (1 1/4 miles) and, after passing through a village, you will arrive at Yeh Pulu.

This is simply a frieze about 40 m (120 ft) long, carved in the rock on one side of the path. It depicts men on horses in a hunting scene. It is strangely dynamic and forceful; there is an energy and a simplicity here that vanishes from later Balinese work where the emphasis is on poise and sublimity. These carvings at Yeh

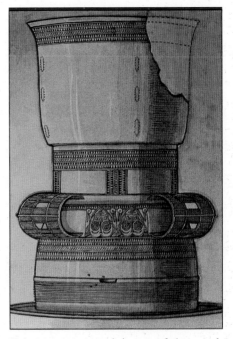

Pulu are more reminiscent of the rough but vigorous work of archaic Greek sculpture, heroic and independent of the requirements of a later orthodoxy. They are thought to date from the fourteenth century. A short walk between rice fields is necessary from where the road ends.

Around Ubud. OPPOSITE: the great rock tombs at Gunung Kawi are mysterious in origin. Situated on the valley floor of the Pakrisan River, they are probably a thousand years old and thus date testify to a formal culture on the island long before the Majapahit invasion. ABOVE: an early twentieth century drawing of the great drum of Pejeng.

ELEPHANT CAVE

Back at the crossroads, take the road toward Ubud and after 1 km (5/8 mile) or so you will arrive at the popular **Goa Gajah** or Elephant Cave.

Visitors to the *goa* might be excused for thinking the place had received an excess of publicity. Coachloads of sightseers unload every day to stumble through a really very small cave, knock their heads

Durga, destructive mother and consort of Siwa. In front of the cave are some large baths, with six standing figures holding bowls from which water pours. They are a testimony to past splendor and are basically in good condition; they could easily be restored.

Some fifty steps lead down from the temple compound that contains the cave and baths to a pleasant natural amphitheater where ponds and a small altar to the Buddha enhance the natural serenity of

against the roof in the inadequate light and stare at a single smallish sculpture (of Ganesa, elephant-headed son of Siwa) illuminated by an oil lamp. Yet the usual array of *warung* and souvenir stalls is assembled and a charge of Rp100, with another Rp200 for the hire of a sarong, is made as if this were one of the island's greatest splendors.

Even so, the man-made cave does date back to the eighth century, and the carving around the cave's rectangular entrance is indeed marvelous, a typically boss-eyed monster appearing to prize open the rock with his fingertips. The statue to the left of the cave entrance is of

the area. As neither Buddhas nor elephants have ever been native to Bali, the site as a whole is something of a historical mystery. Various explanations have been offered as to why the cave is designated Elephant, none of them very satisfactory.

From Goa Gajah it is 5 km (3 1/8 miles) back to Ubud, turning right at Teges where you meet the road coming up from Denpasar.

BANGLI

Bangli is a small town (though referred to up in Penelokan as a "city") on the border of the central and eastern regions, 14 km

(8 3/4 miles) from Gianyar. Bemo fare Gianyar-Bangli is Rp250.

The small hotel and restaurant – **Artha Sastra** (rates: inexpensive) – situated just where the bemos stop, is actually the old palace of the former king of Bangli. A photograph of the young rajah, with two attendants, hangs on the walls of the verandah where lunch is served. It was apparently taken as recently as 1950. Together with the gorgeous doorways and faded gilt mirrors, it provides a key to the atmosphere of a former world. Lewis Carroll's Alice could have slipped through a time warp and been there in a trice, you feel. Yet a glimpse into the once-great rooms reveals camping furniture, and a table with shampoo and a toothbrush.

Bangli's main temple is **Pura Kehen**. Carvings of trumpeting elephants welcome you to the flight of 38 steps leading up to a highly ornate gateway. The whole temple is built in tiers up a steep slope, and its obligatory banyan tree is vast. Otherwise there is little of interest, but the whole is austerely imposing for all that. It was the state temple of the old kingdom of Bangli.

Bangli is also the site of Bali's major psychiatric hospital, something romantic attitudes to the island would have you believe shouldn't exist. Laid out in large grounds with ornate gardens, it looks from the outside a model of progressive thought. But prying visitors are the last thing anyone connected with the place needs.

THE HEIGHTS

PENELOCAN

The mountain area is most dramatically first seen if you arrive there at **Penelokan**. The main road up to this superb vantage point is the one through Bangli, and nothing is seen of the country you are approaching as you ascend until you pass through a ceremonial gateway and everything is suddenly laid out before you.

Turn right here, where the road swings left having finally achieved the crater rim, and take a seat in the cafe of the **Lake View Homestay** (rates: inexpensive) and admire the serenely beautiful spectacle.

What you are actually looking at is a vast caldera, 11 km (6 7/8 miles) across, the hollowed-out remains of a gigantic volcano that in prehistoric times exploded, blowing away its entire cone and leaving only the bony, saucer-shaped rim on which you're sitting. It's as if you are in the back row of

a circus that's in the process of being dismantled; you are looking down at the ring unaware of the giant big-top tent that once stretched from just behind your seat to a point high above you.

Mount Batur, whose broken crest rises 1,717 m (5,633 ft) above sea level, is central to the view. Its slopes are scarred with lava-flows, and all around is a scene of lonely splendor and desolation. Magnificent though the mountain is, it is

OPPOSITE: one of the stone fountains in Goa Gajah (the Elephant Cave) – "they could easily be restored"; ABOVE: Lake Batur. The lake lies within the crater of the volcanic Mount Batur, and the distant skyline is the crater rim.

the product of more recent and smaller eruptions and its summit is actually only 328 m (1,066 ft) higher than the outer-crater rim at Penelokan.

The volcano is not to be underestimated, however. Its last major eruption in 1926 completely destroyed the village of Batur, situated at that time on the western shore of the lake. It was never rebuilt, but its important temple was relocated up on the outer-crater rim, between Penelokan and Kintamani, and this is now the place meant by Batur Village.

To your right lies **Batur Lake**, 492 m (1600 ft) below you. It is 8 km (5 miles) long and 3 km (1 7/8 miles) wide and fills almost a third of the area of the caldera. The cliffs that fall abruptly down to the lake's eastern edge rise to their maximum height in the summit of Mount Abang, 3,153 m (10,250 ft) and in a direct line between Batur and Agung.

The right-hand (eastern) shore of the lake appears to press right up against these cliffs, but long ago some Bali Aga remnants, retreating in the face of invaders, found a flat piece of land and established the village of Trunyan, where few could be interested in following them. The village is clearly visible, a prominent patch of red in an otherwise pastel landscape played over by the changing shadows of the clouds.

At your feet the road zigzags down from Penelokan, branching right to Kedisan on the lake's edge immediately below you, and continuing across the lava flows to the hot springs of Air Panas, about halfway along the left-hand shore. It is possible to spend the night at the Penelokan, accommodation;Lake View-Lake View, but if you have the ascent of Batur in mind you would be better advised to stay at the springs.

Washing cattle in Lake Batur. K'tut Tantri's book *Revolt in Paradise* contains a description of cattle being drowned as ritual sacrifices in this lake. The upland central area of the island is much cooler than the coastal region; it's frequently in cloud and suffers heavy rainfall.

AIR PANAS – HOT SPRING

The road to Air Panas is good, if bumpy. The springs themselves have not been developed and consist merely of a communal bathing pool where the hot water runs into the lake. You can sit in the water at sunset in the company of fifty-odd villagers, some of them scrubbing their washing on the side. It's nicer, though, to swim in the lake itself which the waters

of the spring make very warm at this point.

There are several *losmen* here, all inexpensive, and one hotel. This is the **Balai Seni Toyabungkah** (rates: moderate), the headquarters of the International Association for Art and the Future.

Founded in 1973 by the celebrated Indonesian novelist Sutan Takdir Alisjahbana (born in 1908 and author of over thirty books on philosophy, linguistics, culture and education; his novels include *Endlessly Dogged by Misfortune, The Lamp That Never Failed* and *The Girl in the Robbers' Nest*), it has been the venue for painting contests, mythic dramas and writers' conferences. The author actually

lives there but is frequently away in Jakarta where he holds a professorship.

As a hotel guest you are most likely to engage with the center's artistic aims through the regular dance performances given there by a local troupe. There is also a library containing a range of books on art in several languages. Generally, though, the place isn't a hive of activity, not surprisingly when you consider its remote location. But the atmosphere is pleasant, with guitar music issuing from the stereo in the restaurant, and the setting among flowering trees with a view down to the lake is picturesque.

The road continues beyond Air Panas to **Songan** where there is an attractively sited temple up a track to your left in the center of the village.

THE ASCENT OF BATUR

There's no need for a guide unless you plan to set off in the dark to see the sun rise; in this case you will need to start at 3:30 am and can easily find a guide by asking around at Air Panas.

An early start is advisable anyway, though, not because of the distance but because of the heat later in the day. The Balai Seni serves breakfast from about 6:30 am.

From Air Panas, take the lane that leads toward the mountain from the center of the village. Anyone will point it out to you if you say, "*Batur – jalan jalan*" ("Batur – walking"). It curves gently round to the left until, after about 1 km (5/8 mile), you reach a temple. Pass the temple, continuing on the very clear track, and follow it as it winds across the now cindery scrubland around the base of the mountain. After crossing the second of two (usually dry) river beds, the path turns upwards, heading directly for the peak.

Next comes a steep, dusty bit where valuable assistance is provided as handholds by some small pine trees. At the top is an orange refuse bin that marks the junction of the track with another coming up from the left. From here the path crosses a level stretch and then diverges into several subsidiaries, all making for the ridge on the right. Once you have achieved this, the path becomes unified again and runs clearly ahead of you toward the summit. Views back over the lake are superb.

As you climb, Agung begins to appear behind you above the rim of the outer crater to the east.

the tough grass. Make for two small pines.

Finally you arrive at the high point of the crater rim, the pinnacle that has been ahead of you most of the way up, and here there are two orange refuse bins to prove it.

You are here standing on the top of the high crest that rises so impressively on the right of the volcano when viewed from Penelokan.

The round-crater route is narrow but well trodden. It is not, however, for the

Around the Crater Rim

After a time, the path divides, one branch carrying on straight ahead, the other leading off to the left. Take the left-hand branch for the gentler ascent. This will take you to a low point on Batur's crater rim and with any luck you will encounter local boys offering cold drinks. Considering the distance they have come and the weight they have had to carry, it's only charitable to buy one, and for only a little less than the price they ask.

From here the round-crater path rises steeply to the right. The ground is sandy and loose and in fact most comfortably negotiated barefoot. The wind sings in

faint-hearted. At least at one point the track crosses a very narrow ridge, with steep falls on either side and steam issuing out of the rocks just below. Anyone with a fear of heights will not need to be told to keep away.

An Eerie Silence

The crater itself is an awesome place, with steam rising silently from several clefts

OPPOSITE: a wayside meditating figure; ABOVE: Mount Batur from the crater rim. The volcano erupted in 1917 and then again in 1926, on the second occasion destroying the ancient village of Batur on the shore of the lake.

and giving rise to lush vegetation on the cliffs immediately above. As water is not a constituent element of the inner earth, and this is steam not smoke, the hot vapor must be caused by water percolating down from the surface and boiling on contact with the molten lava below. What is eerie is that the steam rises without sound, and the silence is broken only by the twitter of birds and the occasional ominous sound of a falling stone. At its center the crater is extraordinarily deep, and sheer. The steam rises not only from a vent near the bottom, but also from high up, close to the crater rim.

The descent on the route toward Kedisan begins a little way further round to the left from where you first attained the crater coming up from the springs, at the next bin in fact. The path descends steeply and unpleasantly in a continuous incline to the plain. This is a common ascent route but inferior to the one from Air Panas because its steepness is unrelieved. You are rewarded on arrival at level ground by a small *warung* where you can buy softdrinks and small cakes; sometimes the *warung* is unmanned and you are invited to leave the money due in a box. (The owner is said to be a trained *leyak*, or witch, and to be well aware when his dues have not been paid, and by whom.)

ACROSS THE LAKE

The boats leave across the lake for the Bali Aga village of Trunyan from **Kedisan**. Here the **Segara Homestay and Restaurant** (rates: inexpensive), on the right immediately before you get to the ferry terminal, will provide lunch and, if necessary, rooms.

Arranging your crossing to Trunyan can be difficult. There are official rates, advertised at an official booking office, but there are no regular ferries to take you. Instead, you have to charter a boat, and this means in practice negotiating a price with the skipper. Individuals have little

alternative but to wait for a group planning to charter a boat to come along and then make arrangements to join them.

You will hear preposterous prices quoted for chartering a boat up in Penelokan, as for many other things; at the lakeside they are more reasonable, if you're determined and if you're prepared to wait. Something between Rp10,000 and 15,000 return for a group of three or four is reasonable, and this should include both a visit to the cemetery at Kuban (a short distance from Trunyan but accessible only by boat) and a visit across the lake to the hot springs if you haven't already been there.

TRUNYAN

The trip across takes around half an hour. The donations that are the theme of any visit to the Bali Aga village of Trunyan begin at the quay. Then a group of children, who must be employed fulltime on the project (despite their insistent requests for pens "for school") will attach themselves to you and lead you to the temple where you will be shown a building housing an especially large statue that you will not be allowed to see. From there, the children will lead you around some pigsties, past some hostile-looking adults (though this may be all part of the act) and back to your boat, where they will finally strip off and offer to dive for coins. This they do with remarkable skill. As you leave, they wave and even shout goodbye, the first cheerful acts they have performed throughout the routine.

As you pull up at the little beach serving the cemetery, a reception committee of two solicits a "donation" and presents you with a register for signature. The place of the dead is on the right. The point about

---

Trunyan cemetery where the village dead are laid out on the surface of the earth to decompose. These skulls have been placed at the cemetery entrance to elicit donations from foreign tourists. Small contributions will be quickly removed as setting a bad example.

Trunyan is that they neither cremate nor bury their dead but lay them out to decay in the open air and be picked clean by the forces of nature. Consequently you enter the designated territory with some trepidation. It's not clear exactly what horrors the tourist is allowed to see in periods shortly following on a death, but when I was there, there were merely seven or eight wicker tents containing in some cases a skull, more often just some bones and scraps of clothing, plus some funeral gifts

such as a Sprite bottle or a few hundred rupiah coins.

A small group of skulls placed on a ledge near the entrance marks the spot where a further donation is requested. And in the same way that the donation register you sign on the beach, in common with almost all such registers in Bali, shows only previous donations of several thousands of rupiahs, so, on the same principle, any small notes you donate as you enter the cemetery itself have been removed, as setting a bad example, by the time you leave.

Back to Kedisan
It used to be claimed that boatmen on the lake were in the habit of stopping in the middle and demanding an increase in the

fare. The existence of an official box-office seems to have curbed this custom at least, and simple requests as you approach the landing-stage back at Kedisan should be treated on their merits. The appeals may sound slightly threatening in a way they are not meant to be as the only relevant English phrase the boatmen knows is likely to be a rather blunt-sounding "More money." But the truth is he's only asking for a tip.

CLIMBING ABANG

Back up at Penelokan and again facing the view, you have the alternative of either going round the rim left in the direction of Kintamani and Penulisan, or right and attempting the ascent of Mount Abang.

If you decide on the latter, follow the road down as if you were going back again to Bangli, and take the second turning on the left immediately after the road begins to drop down from the ridge (the first left leads to a restaurant). It's only a few meters down, and there's a shop on the corner but no sign. This road quickly leads back onto the outer-crater rim, but now running east. After 4 km (2 1/2 miles), the main section of the road peels off to the right and descends, eventually to Besakih. The road along the rim continues for another kilometer or so, passes a couple of *warung*, skirts to the right of a small temple, descends a hill, then turns right. There is a house nearby. From this point on you have to walk. The path is well defined but slippery, and it's about two hours to the summit, which is marked by a temple (there's another about halfway up).

BATUR AND KINTAMANI

Going west along the rim of the caldera from Penelokan, you pass two notable restaurants, the **Puri Selera** (rates: moderate) and then the **Kintamani Restaurant** (rates: average and above). As these restaurants depend largely on tourists visiting the crater rim during the

day but going on elsewhere, or back to their hotels, for the evening, they are only open at lunchtimes.

The **Temple of Ulan Danu** at Batur only dates from 1926 when its predecessor down on the shore of the lake was destroyed. Like all temples in Bali, it faces the mountains, in this case the one that was responsible for its destruction. Its situation, of course, is magnificent, and to watch the gorgeously clad celebrants processing round the outside of its walls on its festival days, the wild country of mountain and lake contrastingly pale in the background, is to see something both wonderful and sad – life struggling to placate insensibility – and very much of the essence of Bali.

The best place to stay in Kintamani (virtually continuous with Batur) is several hundred meters off the road to the right. The **Puri Astina** (rates: moderate) has some rather ordinary rooms, and a few better ones commanding a view of the volcano. There is also a bar and a restaurant.

PENULISAN

After Kintamani the road continues to Penulisan and is one of the loveliest in the island, temperate in vegetation now on account of the altitude, and luxuriant on account of the heavy rainfall. It's like an English country road in summer, but forever in leaf.

The temple at Penulisan, **Pura Tegeh Koripan**, is the highest in Bali. Three hundred and thirty-three steps lead from the road up to this easily achieved view-point. Few people visit the temple and there is no commercialization whatsoever. The atmosphere at the top is secluded and quiet, as mossy and crumbling as a Victorian churchyard. The air is scented from the various bushes that sprout on all sides and rather obscure the view – which is spectacular to the north, with the coast and the blue sea lying far below you almost at your feet, and exten-

sive but less well defined to the south. The air is fresh, and this is a wonderful place to sit and think. It's almost certain no one will disturb you.

For all Kintamani's rather scruffy ambiance, and Penelokan's desered reputation for excessive hustling, these crater-rim villages ending in Penulisan are remarkable places, perched on a narrow volcanic ridge with barely room for more than the one main street. They haunt the imagination when many a more pretentious settlement has long been forgotten.

BESAKIH

The road from Penelokan to Besakih begins along the route to Abang (see CLIMBING ABANG, (p.158). This first section has magnificent views down to the left through the trees to the lake and volcano below. After the turn-off to the right it becomes steeper and potholed. The road has been tarred at some time in the past but has deteriorated and is now broken in several places. It poses no problems, though – it is just not a route for fast drivers.

The road descends along a giant spur, affording wonderful views of Agung to the left in good weather. At **Menanga**, turn left for Besakih (6 km, or 3 3/4 miles). After a kilometer or so of descent, the road crosses the River Yehunda across a wooden bridge, replacing one destroyed by the 1963 eruption of Agung. On the right of the road just before the bridge is the Besakih, accommodation; Arca Valley Inn **Arca Valley Inn** (rates: inexpensive), a modern restaurant but no longer offering accommodation.

From here on the road ascends steadily toward Besakih. As you approach, a sliproad leads off uphill to the left. If you take this road you will arrive nearer the central area of the temple than if you go straight on to the official entrance, though the latter approach is the more spectacular, being a processional avenue along the temple's major alignment. Taking the left-hand route, you arrive at a car park on your left (where you must leave your car) followed by a mass of food and souvenir stalls and more permanent shops. Beyond these is the temple.

The Mother Temple of Besakih is the oldest and the largest in Bali. There are precincts for all the sects of Hinduism and for all the old Balinese kingdoms. Thousands of pilgrims visit Besakih every day of the year, and in former times the old kings made annual

receive the offerings, sprinkle the pilgrims three times with holy water as they offer up flowers, also three times, and place clusters of wet rice grains on each temple and on the brow in such a way that they remain there for some time. The Brahmanic *pedanda*, or high priests, only appear for the great ceremonies, though they can regularly be seen at cremations sitting in their high lofts chanting their mantras and wafting incense to the gods.

pilgrimages with their courts to the temple.

The temple is constructed over a mass of terraces that ascend what are in fact the lower slopes of Mount Agung, and of course this is the Mother Temple because Mount Agung is Bali's highest mountain. The various courtyards and enclosures are connected by flights of steps, and it is these, together with the tall, multi-storied *meru* that, with Agung rising steeply immediately behind the central enclosures, make the whole prospect of Besakih so very impressive.

The day-to-day business of the temple is run by the *pemangku*, easily identifiable by their white clothes. They

The main temple complex, or Pura Panataran, at Besakih (there are other, subsidiary ones, especially away to the right) consists of six walled courts, each higher up the mountain than the last. Before you reach the first of these, there is a small walled shrine containing a seven-tiered *meru* on your right – this is the original shrine of the temple.

The wide central staircase, flanked on each side by seven rising stone platforms

The Mother Temple at Besakih. All Balinese temples are oriented towards the mountains, and this, the island's premier place of worship, is sited right on the lower slopes of Agung, Bali's highest summit.

each carrying six carved figures, leads to the first large court. It contains the usual pavilions for offerings, *gamelan* orchestras and the like. The second court is similar but contains three ceremonial chairs sited on a high stone platform known as a *padmasana*, or world-shrine, intended for the three major manifestations of God – Siwa, Wisnu and Brahma. The other courts follow on up rather fewer steps and contain many of the thatched *meru* that are so very characteristic of the temple.

peacefulness here in this cooler, wooded area overlooking the coastal plains.

As so often in Asia, the presence of items from modern life – cigarettes, radios broadcasting advertisements for hair conditioner – act as authenticating devices for religious observances. There is no trace of the idea, common in the West, that antiquity and sanctity go hand in hand, no trace of the idea that the modern is faintly vulgar. There is nothing antiquarian about the religion of the Balinese.

Under the Volcano

The Mother Temple was, not surprisingly, badly damaged at the time of Agung's 1963 eruption, but has been entirely rebuilt. The eruption occurred just as the most extensive and important of all Bali's many rituals, the once-in-a-hundred-years Eka Dasa Rudra, was about to be performed. Details of the events at that traumatic time in Balinese history can be found in Anna Mathews' *The Night of Purnama* (1965) – see BIBLIOGRAPHY for details.

The countryside around the temple is especially lovely. Mandarin oranges grow everywhere, and there is a sense of relaxed

THE ASCENT OF AGUNG

Besakih is a popular place from which to begin the attempt on Mount Agung – but "attempt" is the key word: it is not an easy task. Though the climb there and back can be done in a day if a very early start is made, it is better to go prepared to spend a night on the volcano.

A guide is essential as the early part of the route winds through fields, but more importantly because, if an accident were to occur, it is vital to have someone capable of going back quickly and organizing help. It is relatively easy to find a guide in Besakih – the following took me up and can be recommended: Wayan Pasak, Dalam Puri, Besakih. He is the owner of one of the *warung* at a car park on the left of the upper (left-hand) road leading to Besakih, about 1 km (5/8 mile) before the Mother Temple. Rp15,000-20,000 is a reasonable fee.

For the climb you will need to take with you a flashlight and plenty of food and water, and to wear stout boots and, of course, a hat.

come worn smooth by frequent use; at other times there are only thorny briars – these should not be touched. A night ascent means the temperature is reasonable and there is little problem with insects, but you should choose a date when there is a full, or fullish, moon.

First light comes shortly before 5 am, and is marked by the instantaneous eruption of bird song. This wonderful moment is followed some half hour later by sun-

The trail ascends right through the center of the Mother Temple itself, ascending 34 steps and then turning right and going up the broad lane between the central complex and the large one immediately to its right.

The Climb Begins

After initial meandering (not apparent until you see it in daylight) the path begins to climb. It rises, virtually straight now, up the crest of a long spur, through lush temperate forest. It's earthy underfoot, and on the steeper sections becomes slippery. Handholds are often needed, and some well-placed branches have be-

light appearing on the plains behind you, with the triangular shadow of the mountain dramatically across the landscape. This shadow shortens as the early morning advances and, soon after, the trail itself is sunlit.

The wooded ravines falling away precipitously on either side of you, only dimly discernible in moonlight, are now brilliantly and breathtakingly illuminated.

On Agung: ABOVE: the first rays of dawn strike the mountain; OPPOSITE: struggling up the loose terrain above the tree-line in the greyness of first light.

The Door of Agung

The Door of Agung is where the ridge the trail climbs joins onto the central stock of the volcano. At the point of contact there is a steep area of loose black ash where progress is difficult, but it doesn't last long. Another short ridge takes you to the Door, on the right.

At the Door of Agung, large slabs of rock overlook some broad ledges where it is possible to camp (though there is no water), and indeed various useful items

such as cooking pans are often left there. There are also shrines and the remains of offerings. The rock faces themselves have been painted with the names of innumerable visitors, many of whom attempt the ascent no further than this spectacular point. The view over southern and western Bali is extensive, though the lack of any other mountains close by makes it less than spectacular. Clouds frequently drift by beneath you.

From here to the summit is another two to three hours' climb across terrain that is partly firm, partly ash. The peak you reach is actually the highest point on the mountain, but you cannot see the crater itself from there as it lies accross unstable and dangerous terrain further to the east.

Klungkung. ABOVE: hand-painted movie posters; OPPOSITE: part of the "floating palace", Kertha Gosa. Klungkung has the charm of an Indonesian country town little touched by the tourist influx that has innundated nearby locations.

The descent is hardly preferable to the ascent. The unrelievedly steep and earthy track makes going down, grasping for dear life at trees while your feet shoot away from under you, both very tiring and agony for the toes. You'll not want to waste much time if you hope to be back in Besakih before dark (5:45 pm).

From Sebudi

If your aim is to see down into the crater of Agung, it is far better to make the ascent not from Besakih but from Sebudi. Take the road to Selat, east of Rendang, and ask from there. Again, a guide is advisable as the path is not well marked. Sebudi is a small village so it might be a good idea to fix up with a guide in advance rather than rely on someone being available whenever you happen to chance by.

RENDANG TO KLUNGKUNG

From Rendang, south of Besakih, a most attractive road runs east then south through Selat and Sidemen to Klungkung.

Not far out of Rendang there is a high, tapering barn-like building on the right of the road. This is for drying tobacco.

Iseh has had its share of artists and writers living there but is itself of little interest. What constitutes the attraction of this area of Bali is the countryside itself, rice terraces with forest above them and Mount Agung on the skyline. This steeply hilly countryside is reminiscent of the Massif Central of France, or mid-Wales.

At **Sidemen** there is a modern dam across the river, several new out-of-town houses, children who ask for money and the feeling that the idyll has come to an end. But the road continues down via **Sukat** through very pleasant country, until the gradient lessens and you find yourself entering the ancient provincial capital of Klungkung (see EAST BALI P.166).

BEDUGUL

Fifteen kilometers (9 3/8 miles) west of Kintamani and 51 km (31 7/8 miles) north of Denpasar, Bedugul is a lakeside mountain resort that provides welcome relief from the heat, and especially the humidity, of the coast.

Lake Braton, together with Lakes Buyan and Tambingan, occupies what is in fact another huge caldera, comparable to Batur's, but in this case the northern walls have slipped seawards and it is consequently neither as distinct nor anything like as impressive.

Ulu Danu

At Candikuning on the edge of the lake (which is in places 35 m or 115 ft deep) stands the **temple** of Ulu Danu, set in delightful gardens. Temple buildings occupy two minute offshore islets, and these, with their three- and eleven-tier *meru*, are, hardly surprisingly, much photographed. The temple is dedicated to the spirits that control the irrigation systems that derive their waters from the lake; there are also Buddhist and Islamic temples close by.

It is possible to be taken by rowing boat on a lake trip lasting approximately 45 minutes to see a cave and visit the **Bedugul Hotel and Restaurant** (rates: moderate). Water skiing and parasailing are on offer – contact the hotel for details. Accommodation and meals can also be had at the **Bali Handara Country Club** (rates: average and above) which boasts a golf course.

There is a track encircling the lake, and the walk takes about three hours.

For a guide, ask at the temple for I. Ketut Sudiana, who speaks several languages.

Botanical Gardens

Half a kilometer from the lake along the road back towards Denpasar, by a flower and vegetable market, a road runs off to the right to the Botanical Gardens (admission Rp100; open daily 8 am until 4.30 pm).

The gardens consist of an open area of wooded parkland still in an early stage of development. Pathways have been established, and the clearly labeled trees, on this south-facing, upland slope, are very fine in themselves. Flowers are being added gradually.

At the moment it's a place for quiet, rather extensive walks among glades, with views up to the wooded hills, and, on a weekday at least, almost total solitude. On an island where a huge variety of tropical and subtropical plants, both native and introduced, flourish with ease, the potential here is clearly immense.

EAST BALI

KLUNGKUNG

Thirty-nine kilometers (24 3/8 miles) east of Denpasar lies the former royal capital of **Klungkung.** It's the place you can change bemos for Besakih to the north and for Padangbai, Candi Dasa and Amlapura to the east. The fare from Denpasar to Klungkung is around Rp700.

The town has a cozy feeling to it – there is an extensive market, some good shops, one passable hotel (see WHERE TO STAY below), and a famous monument.

This last is the **Kertha Gosa**, the courthouse of the old kingdom of Klungkung. It consists of two buildings, an elegant little "floating palace" – really just a raised and much-decorated pavilion set in the middle of a wide moat and originally used as a retreat for the judges – and the actual court, raised high for all to see on your left as you enter from Jalan Untung Surapati.

The dreadful punishments said to be reserved for sinners in another life are vividly illustrated on the roof of the little court – mothers who refused to suckle their young being forced to give the breast to a poisonous fish, confirmed bachelors being savaged by a wild boar etc. These pictures are not in fact very old but are copies of the originals made on asbestos some forty years ago.

Everything is very delicate, not least the worn red-brick floor, and the only pity is that the whole compact complex, so restful in design, is sited so very close to Klungkung's main road intersection. But this was the whole point: the open-sided court was not only raised up high but set

temple attached, reached down a few steps from the restaurant.

Shopping

The **market**, to the right of Jalan Diponegoro, is extensive and, like most-Asian markets, all over by early afternoon. By contrast, the **food stalls** close to the bemo terminus just off Jalan Gajah Mada flourish for several hours beginning at sunset. The **shops**, which extend along the two above-mentioned streets

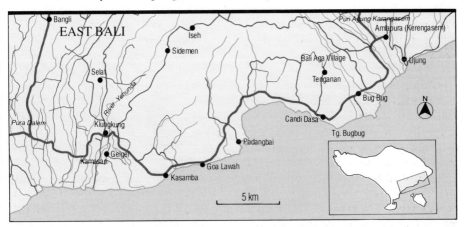

at the very center of the town, open, public and for all to see. Somewhere quieter among the water lilies was set aside for the judges – high priests (*pedanda*) from the Brahmana caste – to consider their judgments.

Both buildings are intricately carved, and the stone animals supporting the pillars in the courthouse itself are particularly noteworthy.

Entrance is Rp200 by a ticket obtainable from the car park opposite. The monument is open from 7 am to 5 pm daily.

Where to Stay

The only hotel in Klungkung that is at all satisfactory is the **Ramayana Palace Restaurant and Hotel** at 152 Jalan Diponegoro (© Klungkung 44; rates: inexpensive). The owner, Nyoman Gede, speaks excellent English, and there is a rather large

from the Kertha Gosa, are surprisingly sophisticated for such a relatively small place – quality batik and temple umbrellas are among the Balinese specialties that can be found.

Klungkung itself is a combination of a quiet country town and a very Oriental-market. Marigolds piled by their thousands on blue tarpaulins, groups of girls skinning tiny mauve onions, bemos arriving from all parts, patent scorpion medicines being sold at the curbside, the harsh glare of kerosene lamps as corn cobs are toasted and yesterday's hits from Jakarta jangle out from a mobile juke box, a post-cremation *angklung* (processional *gamelan*) in the intensely hot afternoon – Klungkung may have only the one monument but it is a fascinatingly typical Balinese town, attractive in a way Denpasar no longer is, and its atmosphere little diluted by the impulse to cater to the foreign needs and tastes of tourists.

GELGEL AND KAMASAN

Directly to the south of Klungkung, leaving the town by Jalan Puputan, are the villages of Gelgel and Kamasan. Gelgel is the old, pre-eighteenth-century capital of the area and, though it was ravaged by lava in 1963, the old **Royal Temple** still stands. Pottery-making can also be seen. Kamasan is the center for a traditional style of painting. (See PAINTING in THE CULTURE OF BALI.)

THE COAST ROAD

From Klungkung, the main road east to Amlapura (almost universally known by the Balinese as Karangasem) runs down to the coast. You leave town along Jalan Diponegoro, passing the Ramayana Palace Hotel on your right, and cross the River Unda by a high bridge.

During the eruption of Mount Agung in 1963, a former bridge was destroyed by the lava coming down the river valley, and a few kilometers out of Klungkung extensive lava fields can be seen to the right of the road. The lava flowed seawards in two arms, this one to the west and another, following the valleys of the rivers Buhu, Banka and Njuling, to the east. Both Amlapura, which stands on the banks of the Njuling, and Klungkung were thus lucky to escape serious damage.

After 7 km (4 3/8 miles), the road runs through **Kusamba's** main street. This is the small market and fishing village from which boats leave for Nusa Penida and Nusa Lembongan;access by boat from KusambaNusa Lembongan. To reach the sea, fork right at the far (or eastern) end of the village, where a building stands in the middle of the road. A lane runs straight to the beach past a mosque and a school. Ask at the last *warung* on the right about boats to the islands. Don't, however, expect to be able to leave any later than early afternoon: waves tend to build up in the Badung Strait during the day and by mid-afternoon landing on the beach at Kusamba – there is no jetty – becomes dangerous. The one-way fare in a wooden motorized *prahu* is normally Rp1,500, and the trip takes around three hours.

The crossing can also be made in rather larger boats that hold up to 25 passengers. To find these boats, go 1 km (5/8mile) along the main road in the direction of Amlapura and turn right down Jalan Pasir Putih. (There is a little sign on the left of the main road indicating the turning with the words "Dermaga Penyebrangan Kusamba 200 m"). In addition, see the NUSA PENIDA section for information on the speedboat ferry from Padangbai.

Bat Cave

A couple of kilometers east of Kusamba is the extraordinary **Goa Lawah**. It's only a relatively small opening in the limestone cliff, but it is the home of what appear to be hundreds of thousands of only semi-nocturnal bats. A temple has been built immediately in front of its entrance, and so it's necessary to pay a donation of Rp200, in return for the loan of a scarf.

It isn't really possible to enter the cave as the low roof is completely covered in bats and the floor coated in a thick layer of guano. Several shrines stand just inside the cave, also guano-crowned. But there's no need to go in to see the bats at close quarters – they crowd together over large areas of the outside walls and it is easy to get a camera to within half a meter of them. Hanging upside down in full daylight, they twist their necks and peer at you as you approach, preparing no doubt for flight. With the massed squeaking, the crowds of kneeling devotees, the

---

Goa Lawah. Because the home of so many bats has been considered sacred, a temple has been built there and throughout the day a stream of devotees arrives, many bearing offerings as in this photograph. But the temple is as interesting as the bats, and the juxtaposition of the two is nothing less than astonishing.

incense, the priests' prayers and the flashing of tourists' cameras, it's at one and the same time grotesque, comic and wonderful. It's situated right on the main road and no one should drive past without sparing five minutes for a quick look, however pressed you are for time, or anxious to get on to the comforts and consolations of Candi Dasa.

Salt from the Sea

Directly over the road from the bat temple, on the black-sand beach, is a primitive salt factory, where salt is procured from sea water. Under a thatched roof water drips down bamboo pipes and a solitary worker displays a bowl of gleaming salt crystals for your admiration. Nusa Penida shimmers along the horizon.

The salt-making process is as follows. Wet sand is spread out on the beach and, when partly dry, is placed in a container inside one of the huts.

Eventually a salty liquid begins to drip out, and this is transferred to long wooden troughs where the last of the water evaporates.

It's almost as interesting – natural but unexpected – as the bats.

PADANGBAI

Eighteen kilometers (11 1/4 miles) from Klungkung is Padangbai, Bali's port of entry for luxury-liner passengers and the terminal for the ferry to Lombok.

Quite what the cruise customers think of the island when they are ferried in to Padangbai's single wharf – large ships cannot come alongside and moor just round the headland in the direction of Candi Dasa – doesn't bear thinking about. The village – for that's really all it is – just consists of a single street running inland from the jetty and a few fishermen's huts. A greater contrast to the luxury of Nusa Dua or Sanur, and presumably the cruise liners, can hardly be imagined.

Yet Padangbai grows on you. It has the attraction of a busy terminal little concerned with tourists most days of the year (traders and hawkers tend to come in from outside when the cruise ships are due). The sandy beach to the east of the jetty is home to many colorful *prahu*, and the sale of the night's catch in the early morning, alongside the boats, is a colorful spectacle. Also, many of Padangbai's inhabitants are Moslems, and to stand on a hillside above the bay at sunset and hear the muezzin's song from the mosque, as a small bird orchestra circles the valley as if in harmony with the words of the Prophet, is to experience something of the Old East preserved almost intact in this strange, beautiful land.

Where to Stay

Much the nicest place to stay in Padangbai is the **Rai Beach Inn** (rates: moderate). It only has four rooms, but each is a self-contained two-story house built entirely of bamboo and wood, with a high arched roof and contained within a little compound. It's on the beach east of the jetty, about halfway along on the way to the headland. Just past it is the **Padangbai Beach Inn** (rates: inexpensive), a simpler affair with a nice outlook over the bay. Neither establishment has a restaurant.

Where to Eat

The best place to eat in Padangbai is **Kendedes Restaurant** (rates: inexpensive) where large portions of well-prepared Western and Indonesian food are served in a friendly atmosphere. There are a couple of other choices, at one of which, **Johnny's** (rates: inexpensive) there is an extraordinarily amusing singing bird.

Ferries to Lombok ...

Ferries for Lombok leave Padangbai three times a day. The departure times are supposedly 9 am, 1:30 pm and 3 pm, but I sat and watched the 1:30 boat pulling away just before 1:15, and it seems advisable to arrive, and board the ship, in plenty of time. Fares are Rp3,500 economy and Rp4,500 first-class, one way. Autombiles are Rp 45,000.

... And Further Afield

Padangbai is also the place for catching a boat to other islands of the world's largest archipelago. Six ships operated by the Pelayaran Nasional Indonesia (PELNI for short) operate biweekly schedules on six different routes. Only one of these ships, the *MV Kelimutu*, calls at Padangbai, but by taking the one-day trip on this vessel, either west to Surabaya on Java, or east to Ujung Pandang on Sulawesi, you can link up, one way or another, with all the other ships. The *MV Kelimutu* leaves Padangbai going east on alternate Wednesdays at noon, and at the same time every other Thursday going west to Surabaya.

A Hidden Cove

Lastly, there is an attractive little cove just round the headland on your right when you're looking out to sea. Turn right immediately after Johnny's Restaurant as you approach the wharf, and then after a couple of hundred meters turn left at the sign for **Biastugel Beach**. The white-sand beach, a ten-minute walk at most from the village and only 150 m (487 ft) wide, is a classic "all to ourselves" location. Not for long, however: a hotel is being built overlooking the tiny cove and will no doubt dominate the scene.

TENGANAN

Immediately before you arrive in Candi Dasa from the west, a road leads off left 4 km (2 1/2 miles) to Tenganan. Motorbikes wait at the junction to take you (Rp200-300).

Tenganan is Bali's foremost example of the social organization of the Bali Aga (see FROM JAVA MAN TO GOLKAR, p.14). It is as friendly, tidy and above all prosperous as Trunyan, the Bali Aga village on Lake

Batur, is hostile, grubby and impoverished.

The prime feature of Tenganan life is that everything is held communally and membership of the community is as a result strictly controlled. As the village is a major landowner in the area, its privileged three hundred or so inhabitants do little menial work and are free to devote their time to weaving, writing on *lontar* leaves, or simply admiring one another's fighting cocks, some of which are dyed

pink. Forms of dance (the *rejang*), ritual fighting (*pandan*), instrumental music (*gamelan selunding*) and ikat cloth (*gringsing*) are found here that occur nowhere else in Bali. Full details can be found in Madi Kertonegoro's *The Spirit Journey to Bali Aga, Tenganan Pegringsingan*, a whimsical and informative book that catches well the genial spirit of the village.

The village looks utterly unlike any other in Bali. The family compounds are

Erotic dalliance is in no way alien to Hindu art; this example from Amlapura compares well with anything that might be happening on Kuta beach after dark.

arranged in long lines on either side of the north-south concourses which rise in successive terraces as they move uphill. Because the compounds each have a pavilion with an overhanging roof immediately inside the external wall, the appearance is given of a street of houses with thatched roofs in, perhaps, the west of England. At the far end is a communal meeting place, the *bale paruman desa*, while the village temple is near the entrance from the road, surrounded by frangipani trees.

The section of the village away to the right (east) is reserved for villagers who have in some way forfeited full membership of the community. It is known as **Banjar Pande**. Here small windmills (*pinengan*, meaning wings) can be seen above the houses, serving no practical purpose but constructed just for pleasure. Up the hill behind Banjar Pande is the cemetery; the Bali Aga here do not expose their dead like their cousins in Trunyan but bury them in the ground in accordance with the practice of the Indra sect of Hinduism.

Lontar

At first sight it looks as if Tenganan is all tourist shops. All the sales activity, however, is concentrated in the first street you come to; in the parallel street to the right there is none at all. All the shops are part of people's houses. In the **Indra Art Shop**, for example, you can take a coffee while the owner, I. Wayan Gelgel, inscribes a motto for you on a *lontar*. First he cuts in the words with a pointed knife, then rubs in a black oil from the burnt *kemiri* nut. He has a collection of old *lontar* books, leaves threaded on a string with bamboo covers. The words are inscribed on one side, illustrations on the other. The texts are old stories from the *Ramayana* (see HEROES AND VILLAINS, p.57). The books are fastened shut with an old Chinese coin, Bali's first money, used now only for ceremonial purposes. The *lontar* leaves have been first boiled in salty rice water to strengthen and preserve them.

The craft shop of I. Nyoman K. Nurati is in the house where the Swiss writer Urs Ramseyer stayed while writing his *Art and Culture of Bali*.

CANDI DASA

Candi Dasa (pronounced *Chandi Dasa*) is a popular white-sand beach 13 km (8 miles) southwest of Amlapura. It is the only beach on this stretch of coast that has experienced any degree of tourist

development, and that only comparatively recently. The name probably means Ten Tombs and refers to some ancient monuments near the village of **Bug Bug** (pronounced *Boog Boog*) 2 km (1 1/4 miles) to the east.

The beach, only 1 km (5/8 mile) long, is moderately attractive, sandy but with patches of coral here and there. Where once the sand sloped gently down to the water, a sea wall has now been built along the whole length of the frontage to enable the construction of hotels on the narrow strip between the coast road and the sea. As a result, at high tide the beach disappears completely, but you can then retreat up the steps to your hotel restaurant, take an iced lemon juice and flick the pits directly into the waves lapping just below you.

Candi Dasa originated in the rage to find a quieter alternative to Kuta in the lower-price bracket, and though the unspoilt ambiance of the early eighties is no more and the entire sea front taken up with accommodation of one sort or another, the place does remain relatively undisturbed. No one (to date) tries to sell you a T-shirt, and you can admire

Beginning at the Klungkung/ Padangbai end and moving east, the **Candidasa Beach Bungalows and Restaurant** (℃ Amlapura 180; rates: moderate) is a standard but attractive beach hotel and the first place you see, when coming in this direction, on the coast side of the road. A little further along is the **Puri Bali** (rates: inexpensive), a simple *losmen* with no restaurant.

The **Puri Pandan** (℃ Amlapura 169; rates: moderate), by contrast, has an ex-

the lovely panorama – a headland to the right, islets to the left and Nusa Penida lying low straight ahead – and perfect your suntan with the minimum of interruption.

Where to Stay

The attraction of Candi Dasa, in fact, is that most of its *losmen* and beach hotels front directly onto the sea, and all the accommodation recommended here enjoys this advantage. There are some twenty places in all and it would be no long job to walk along the beach and take a closer look at the establishments that take your fancy. The following, however, is a sample selection.

cellent restaurant serving first-class Western and Chinese food, unusually good coffee and wonderful icecream. Many visitors from neighboring *losmen* eat and drink here and at night the kerosene-lamp lit restaurant can get quite crowded.

Continuing east, the **Pondok Bambu Seaside Cottages** (℃ Amlapura 169; rates: moderate) is the most sophisticated

Two angles on Candi Dasa. The beach is lined with small hotels along all but the stretch shown ABOVE, while the sign OPPOSITE indicates the way some visitors would like the resort – and Bali as a whole – to develop.

place at Candi Dasa, serving cocktails in would be elegant surroundings. Lastly, the **Amarta Homestay** and the **Natia Homestay** (rates: inexpensive), standing side by side, are excellent value for money and have simple restaurants offering the standard tourist dishes found all over the island.

AMLAPURA (KARANGASEM)

The Balinese usually refer to their main towns by the name of the districts, or *kabupaten*. Denpasar is Badung; Singaraja, Buleleng; and Amlapura, Karangasem. This last substitution is so common that occasionally, even when the name Amlapura is being used, it is listed in alphabetical indexes under the letter *K*. The name Amlapura was only officially adopted after the eruption of Mount Agung in 1963, and Karangasem is still the name on the lips of every bemo conductor touting for passengers heading east in the streets of Klungkung.

The Palace

There is only one place deserving a visit in the town, the palace, but it is somewhere that shouldn't be missed. It also contains one of the nicest places to stay anywhere in Bali.

The various *puri* are really part of one and the same complex and together originally constituted the living quarters of the family of the rajah of Karangasem. Some – the Madhura, for instance – are now virtually taken over by humbler residences that continue, however, to have the air of being within the domain of a palace.

The Puri Amsterdam, with its "floating" pavilion (ie. a pavilion set in the middle of a lake), is still largely intact, however, though unfortunately you can not go inside the main building. Karangasem was one of the old Balinese kingdoms that made an accommodation with the Dutch, and as a result the rajah's family were allowed to retain their former status, at least outwardly. The portraits and other items that can be seen on the verandah of the main building suggest, in their combination of Dutch and Balinese styles, that the interior must have been a stately place indeed. Now cocks, set out in their cages, crow, and otherwise only the click of the rare tourist's camera and the rustle of the wind in the trees break the silence.

From here you can go down through the triple-tiered, red-brick gateway and across the road to inspect even more royal outhouses. Here the problem of knowing whether or not you are in someone's house or an ancient monument becomes acute. The problem is solved by acquiring some of the children who will gather around you as guides; wherever they take you, you can consider yourself "invited." The whole area is extensive, on both sides of the road, and exceptionally delightful because it is quiet, lived-in, and, with its trees and muted elegance, human and touching.

Where to Stay

The **Homestay Balakiran** (rates: inexpensive) is actually part of the Puri Madhura. It's very pretty, your reception dignified yet friendly, and, with the owner a guide too, it's a particularly attractive place to spend a night in this little-visited town.

The owner of the Balakiran can probably be persuaded to show you where you can inspect a local bird orchestra. The doves sit preening themselves in their red and blue cages in a garden overlooking the Moslim village of Nyuling. Bells and flutes of different sizes are fitted on col-

Street scene in Amlapura (Kerangasem). Few tourists venture as far as this, the easternmost town on the island. It has an undisturbed air, and its palace area is curiously inhabited, as if the descendents of royal retainers have now taken over the whole complex.

lars under the birds' ruffs so that the instruments stand out on their chests. They seem perfectly attuned to Amlapura's general ambiance of almost sedate tranquility.

WATER PALACES

One of Amlapura's twentieth-century rajahs constructed two water palaces, one north and the other south of the town. **Tirtagangga** (meaning "Ganges

Water"), 5 km (3 1/8 miles) to the north, is the more frequently visited because it is still more or less in working order, though damaged in the 1963 eruption. You can swim in one of the two pools, eat in a cafe and even stay the night in rooms run by the same management (**Restaurant Tirta-Ayu**; rates: inexpensive). Entrance is Rp200, and another Rp300 to swim. But efficient

ABOVE: a palace gateway, Amlapura; OPPOSITE: part of the ruins of the water palace at Ujung. The original concept envisaged tiers of irrigated gardens descending to ornamental pavilions set in lakes. The remaining, structurally sound terraces can be clearly seen in this picture.

and presumably clean though Tirtagangga is, it does little for the imagination – in total contrast to the other water palace, at **Ujung**.

No bemos run the 3 km (1 7/8 miles) to Ujung and it's necessary to arrange to go by motorbike (Rp500 for the round trip, with additions if you stay long and keep the driver waiting, is about right). But it's well worth the effort.

The site is almost wholly in ruins, but the concept is so magnificent, and the crumbling remains now given over to agriculture so picturesque, that the whole complex leaves an indelible impression on the mind.

Ujung was built with Dutch aid in 1921 but severely damaged by volcanic activity in 1963. It was in the process of being restored (by two Australians who began work in 1974) when it was finally destroyed by an earthquake in 1979. The present descendants of the rajah have tentatively agreed with the government on a restoration program, though at the time of writing no work had yet been undertaken.

A young member of the rajah's family living on the site will act as your guide and will also show you a tattered photograph of the area taken a year before the earthquake. It's quite possible, though, that it's more evocative in its present condition.

Frangipani and palms sprout from among the fallen pillars and make artlessly elegant compositions with the grazing cattle and the one remaining dome. Above the white masonry and its flowering vegetation rise tier after tier of terraces, once gardens, topped at the skyline with further ornamental structures. A walk up steps and then away to the right will lead you to a magnificent carved head from which gushes water, against the background of the foothills of Agung.

That dereliction can have its own distinctive beauty is nowhere in Bali more evident than in the ruined water palace at Ujung.

Off the
Beaten
Track

NUSA PENIDA AND NUSA LEMBONGAN

Nusa Penida lies long and gaunt along the horizon from the east Bali coast, and from Sanur and Benoa its southern cliffs present a magnificently etched spectacle in the late afternoon light. Few tourists, though, ever make it over there.

By contrast, the smaller Nusa Lembongan, a short boat trip from Penida, has

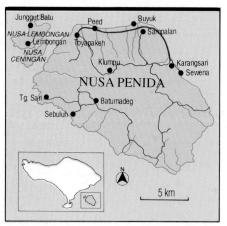

recently become a rather popular venue for surfers and divers. Together the two islands constitute a fine round tour, one arduous, the other restoring. They make a considerable change from "mainland" Bali.

You can go straight to Nusa Lembongan from Sanur. *Prahu* wait on the beach to the left (north) of the Bali Beach Hotel there is no regular service and you must approach one of the skippers and negotiate a price. You should leave Sanur early, especially if you plan to come back the same day, as the boatmen don't like to be out on the Badung Strait after mid-afternoon. The trip takes three hours outward from Sanur, but considerably less going back owing to favorable ocean currents.

You can also, of course, cross over from Nusa Lembongan to Nusa Penida. The inhabitants of the larger island, however, and most of those from Nusa Lembongan as well, take the shorter crossing, via Kusamba or Padangbai.

Motorized *prahu* from Kusamba leave from two places on the beach about a kilometer apart (see the KUSAMBA section of EAST BALI, p. 169 for details of how to locate these departure points). Crossings both ways take place almost wholly in the mornings as the surf at Kusamba tends to get bigger as the day progresses and can make landing and departing difficult, if not dangerous. The one-way fare is Rp1,500 for locals and you may be able to travel for this amount too, though it is normal to charge foreigners some 50 percent more and it is not always a good idea to argue when the fare is so very low anyway. Boats leave when they are full, so how quickly you get away is entirely a matter of chance.

As the crossing takes between two and three hours, you may prefer to take the speedboat service from Padangbai. This leaves several times during the morning, beginning at around 7 am. There is one boat which is moored at Nusa Penida overnight; consequently, you wait on the beach at Padangbai until it arrives on its first trip of the day from the island. Where you wait is immediately to the left (east) of the jetty. The crossing takes forty minutes and the fare is Rp2,000. Crossings later in the morning cannot normally be relied on and the best plan is to spend the night in Padangbai if getting there in the early morning is likely to pose difficulties.

The crossing is 14 km (8 3/4 miles) from Kusamba, marginally further from Padangbai.

Most of the boats from Kusamba arrive on Nusa Penida at Toyapakeh, whereas the speedboat from Padangbai arrives at Buyuk, close to Sampalan, the capital. But it makes little odds which one you arrive at as there are regular bemo services along the coast road and Toyapakeh to Sampalan will take you, at most, 15 minutes.

The spectacularly precipitous south coast of Nusa Penida. That a bamboo stairway should descend these cliffs is scarcely credible.

NUSA PENIDA

A LIMESTONE ISLAND

Nusa Penida is a limestone plateau, 20 by 16 km (12 1/2 by 10 miles) and rising to a height of 529 m (1,735 ft). Being limestone, it's rocky and dry, the rainfall sinking straight into the ground and forming underground caverns. Because of this, the island has always been poor. In the Balinese religious scheme of things it is considered malign, and in earlier times convicts from the kingdom of Klungkung were sent there.

Nevertheless, today it supports a population of around 45,000, agriculture has improved after government assistance in building cisterns to catch the rainwater, and seaweed farming – evidence of which can be seen all along the northern coast – seems very promising. A jetty recently completed at Toyapakeh should boost the economy by allowing large vessels to dock and carry away the seaweed and rock (for the construction industry) which are the island's main products.

Even so, Nusa Penida is a strange place, just as the Balinese feel it is. Foreign visitors are immediately surrounded by crowds of children – and some adults – crying *"Turis! turis!"* (tourist), and inland the roads are rough indeed. Very few people speak any English at all. Nevertheless, the cliffs on the south side of the island are worth a lot of hard traveling to see, and there are a couple of other things worth seeing in the north.

SAMPALAN

Sampalan is the main village on the island, but it has little to show other than a market. The coast road forms its main and almost only street. But it's attractive nevertheless. On a bright morning, its narrow, tree-lined shade crowded with country people is more like eastern Indonesia than anywhere on mainland Bali.

The island's only accommodation for visitors is the very satisfactory **Bungalows Pemda** (rates: inexpensive) at the east end of the village. There are five bungalows, each with two rooms. There is no restaurant and you will have to make do with one of the several *warung* on the main street; don't expect them to be open much after 8 pm.

A CAVE

If you take the coast road on eastwards from Sampalan – and your transport will probably be a truck loaded with goods as well as passengers – you will, after about twenty minutes, reach the site of a large cave, **Goa Karangsari**. It's between Sewana and Karangsari, a couple of hundred meters up from the road on the right. Just say *"goa"* (cave) and all the passengers will tell you when you've arrived.

It isn't strictly necessary to have a guide, but a light of some sort is essential. The odds are you'll hire the two together at the *warung* where the truck will put you down. Nusa Penida has little experience of tourism, but the word has got around that foreigners are rich. Thus the few visitors who do appear are treated as manna from heaven and prices quoted can be laughably high. You will probably end up spending Rp4,000 to be shown around the cave by a guide bearing a powerful kerosene lamp. This is picturesque, but a flashlight would show you considerably more.

Entrance to the cave is through a narrow gap in the rocky hillside, but inside it's spacious, with a high roof and a level, sandy floor. It extends for some 300 m (984 ft), and at the far end you emerge on another hillside overlooking an inland valley supporting only scrub, and with few signs of habitation. About halfway through the cave you pass beneath a colony of bats, and a little further on there is a place where water drips down from the roof and a small shrine has been constructed. There are various side passages but for the most part they peter out without leading to further major features.

PEED

If you take the coast road in the other, western direction from Sampalan you will arrive after ten minutes at the celebrated, or notorious, temple at Peed (pronounced *Ped*). It stands on the right of the road in the village of the same name. It is the home of Bali's sourest deity, Ratu Gede Macaling. The word *macaling* derives from a Balinese word meaning "fang".

According to the tenets of Balinese religion, malign forces must be placated as much as benign ones worshipped, so the temple is crowded with visitors from all over Bali on its *odalan* (feastday). The place itself is large but not especially beautiful. The shrine to Ratu Gede Macaling is in an extension to the northwest of the temple.

ACROSS COUNTRY

The real attraction of Nusa Penida is the dramatic southern coastline. Access, however, is not easy – there is no public transport here and it's necessary to hire someone to take you on a motorbike, or possibly in a four-wheel-drive overland vehicle.

A teacher, Nyoman Lindra, acts as a guide and can easily be contacted at the secondary school at Toyapakeh. He speaks several European languages and some Japanese. He will take you on his motorbike; to charter anything larger, approach the bemo drivers. Lindra asks Rp15,000 for the trip; a bemo might be Rp25,000 for the half day.

The road south branches off the coast road 2 km (1 1/4 miles) west of Sampalan and rises steeply and circuitously to **Klumpu**. Thus far the road is tarred and in good condition. It's after Klumpu that things get difficult. The track rises and falls over rough ground and there are frequent rocky outcrops that have to be negotiated – there are half a dozen places where a pillion rider has to get off and walk. Though generally well drained, there are patches that are slippery after rain.

Bear right at **Batumadeg**, avoiding the road left which leads via Batukandik to the east of the island. The road now is even rougher than before. On both sides are terraces of manioc, corn and occasionally tobacco, where the terrain allows them. The high hills that form the island's center rise to the left. The whole drive, from Sampalan to Sebuluh, takes an hour and a half.

From Sebuluh, a village of thatched houses set in a hollow, it is necessary to walk. A boy can easily be found to take you and will be surprised to receive any payment. Something in the region of Rp500 should nevertheless be offered. You descend into a dry valley, and then up again to the cliff edge, a walk of twenty minutes. Monkeys play in the trees en route.

A CLIFF STAIRWAY

The path arrives at the cliff at the top of a most spectacular and terrifying cliff path. The highest point on this coast, 228 m (750 ft) above sea level, is close to here and this extraordinary aerial stairway, for that is what it is, descends almost the entire distance. It runs diagonally down across the cliff face. It is constructed of bamboo and wood, and though it makes use here and there of natural ledges in the cliff it is elsewhere supported only on trees growing out from the cliff face.

The purpose of this exposed stairway, which no one with the slightest fear of heights should even consider for a moment negotiating, is to enable the villagers of Sebuluh to get down to a place where fresh water gushes out in great profusion a few meters above sea level. In earlier times this was an invaluable source of drinking water during periods of drought. The women would ascend the horrendous route carrying giant buckets of water on their heads, while the men carried two containers apiece slung on either end of a pole. The villagers still go down every 210 days for the *odalan* of the temple down on the rocks at the sea's edge.

The best place to see the whole structure lies 15 minutes' walk to the west. You follow the track down over some terraces to where a turning-off left leads along a deep and grand valley, heavily wooded on the far side, and onto a spur jutting out into the sea and culminating in a small temple. From here you can see the whole extent of the stairway, the water pouring out over a large rock, and the impressive coast to the east.

There are three other such stairways on the south coast of Nusa Penida, known as **Seganing**, **Anceng** and **Swean**. But the one at Sebuluh is the longest.

It is a particular feature of the island that its supply of fresh water, otherwise in such short supply, is situated here at the inaccessible south coast rather than in the north where most of the population lives and where access is easy. But the resulting cliff routes are immensely dramatic and one of the most impressive and extraordinary things to be seen anywhere in Bali. Yet they are almost wholly unknown to travelers.

NUSA LEMBONGAN

Prahu leave Nusa Penida for Nusa Lembongan from Toyapakeh in the mornings. It is important you establish the fare on his route before leaving. They go either around Lembongan to Jungutbatu on the far side, or the shorter distance to the village known simply as **Lembongan**. The fare to Jungutbatu is Rp1,000, to Lembongan somewhat less, for locals at least. In each case the trip takes under an hour. From Lembongan it's a twenty-minute walk to Jungutbatu, and another ten minutes to the beach north of the village where most of the accommodation catering to tourists is to be found.

The brighter, more cheerful aspect of the smaller island is apparent even as you make the crossing. The colorful wooden *prahu* are remarkably stable, though the channel separating the islands is anyway very shallow. Fish dart over the coral and schoolchildren wave as you leave the clouded heights of Nusa Penida behind you.

The southern end of the island manages to attain a few meters in height. From then on it descends to the long sandy spit where the hotels and losmen are situated.

JUNGUTBATU

The beach at Jungutbatu is sandy and faces a reef offering excellent snorkeling and scuba diving. Beyond the reef there is fine surfing too. A wreck to the right, its prow rising from the water like a giant shark's fin, is a prominent feature of the seascape.

Most people come to Jungutbatu direct from Sanur (see the introduction to this section for details). At the time of writing the beach is both relatively quiet and at the same time favored by a somewhat fashionable clientele. With the sun setting center stage and the lights of Sanur's Bali Beach Hotel twinkling at night from far across the strait, it is a very pleasant and relaxing place.

The most expensive hotel here is **Wayan's Nasa Lembongan Bungalows and Restaurant** (rates: moderate). The restaurant is the only one on the beach and is excellent, serving good Western and other food in a glorious, high-roofed structure, the floor of which is the very sand of the beach itself. Bookings can be made via PO Box 37, Denpasar 800001, or by phoning the following numbers in Kuta: 51875 and 51170.

Many visitors choose to stay next door at the **Wayan Tarci Losmen** (rates: moderate). Here guests can eat an inexpensive but excellent communal meal together under the stars. **Johnny's Bungalow** (rates: moderate) and the **Losmen Agung** (rates: inexpensive) provide further rooms. Most people seem to end up in the big restaurant sooner or later.

WEST BALI

THE NATIONAL PARK

Owing to its low rainfall and distance from any other water supply, West Bali has always been very thinly populated. Virtually the only significant settlements are around the coast, and the hilly, scrub-covered interior for the most part comes within the boundaries of the **West Bali**

Conservation (PPHA). Their headquarters is at **Cekik**, 3 km (1 7/8 miles) south of Gilimanuk, the terminal for the ferries from Java. The PPHA has another office south of Denpasar at Jalan Suwung 40 (PO Box 320). There is also an office at Labuhanlalang, 12 km (7 1/2 miles) east of Cekik.

MENJANGAN ISLAND

Labuhanlalang is the site of the jetty for boats to Menjangan Island. The island is

National Park. This was established in 1983, expanding an earlier but much smaller nature reserve set aside by the Dutch.

Trails link the main features of the mainland section of the park. The few who use them are usually nature lovers on the lookout for the rare species thought to be present in the area – the white starling, deer-like *banteng*, and the Balinese tiger. It is now so long since a sighting of this last was reported that it is thought to be, tragically, extinct.

In order to enter the national park it's necessary to have a permit. This can be obtained at any of the offices of the Directorate General of Forest Protection and Nature

within the national park, as is much of the coastal water in the area. The aim of this arrangement is to protect the very fine coral reefs around the island, the best remaining off Bali according to the experts.

Menjangan Island is the main attraction in West Bali. Both snorkeling and scuba diving are possible, but the traveling time from Denpasar (three hours in each direction) makes the day-trips

The coast of West Bali is almost entirely devoid of foreign visitors. In their absence, Balinese with no way of benefitting from the lucrative tourist trade toil away to make a very meagre living from the sea.

advertised by agents in southern Bali a poor option.

ALONG THE COAST

The long coast road offers little interest. Some 8 km (5 miles) before Negara, coming from Tabanan, there is an attractively situated cliff-top temple with frangipani trees at **Rambutsiwi** (turn left down a short side road). And on the northern section, between Gilimanuk and Pura Pulaki (see NORTH BALI, p.103), there are hot springs at **Banyuwedang**, 7 km (4 3/8 miles) east of Labuhanlalang.

BUFFALO RACES

Most visitors come to West Bali in September for the water-buffalo races at **Negara**. Two carts compete at a time, each pulled by two buffaloes. Because the 11 1/2 km (7 1/4 mile) track isn't wide enough for overtaking, there are separate start and finishing lines for each competitor, and the one that crosses its own finishing line first stands a good chance of being declared the winner. Nothing is for certain, however, as "style" as well as speed is taken into account by the judges.

The exact date of the races varies from year to year so consult the Badung Government Tourist Office (✆ 23399 and 23602) in Denpasar if you are in Bali at around that time.

The Balinese of all social classes have a poise and equanimity that bears little relation to their social standing or means of livelihood.

Lastly . . .
the
Earthly
Paradise

WHEN the first Western artists arrived in the thirties, bumping over the rough roads in their early Mercedes, easels piled in the back, and sat staring at one another with a wild surmise on discovering a people who worshiped volcanoes, cremated their dead and performed dance dramas that originated in northern India, they declared Bali a paradise. What exactly did they mean? And can the culture that so excited the minds of those early visitors survive now the island has become a tourist mecca?

What constitutes a "paradise" depends largely on who's looking at it, and more especially what he's looking for. The thirties artists were a mixed bunch, but they were all to some extent fugitives from the materialism of the Western industrialized world. They were looking for a place that had none of the vices of the West, and displayed all the virtues the West lacked. And the reason they judged Bali to be so very special was that they thought that here they'd finally found it.

INFINITY EVERYWHERE

Bali came to represent for that generation not only an idyll where the sun shone forever along palm-lined beaches, but a place where men related to each other and to the universe in ideal ways. Their relations were not commercial but brotherly, their sexual life was unspoilt by repression and guilt, they practiced art naturally and without thought of gain, and their religion harmonized with nature and reconciled the contradictions of good and evil. Above all, they lived their daily lives surrounded by a sense of the infinite in all things.

When these artists saw the Balinese at festival time dancing in their flower-laden temples under the full moon, they saw a people who possessed all the virtues their own societies lacked, who were (they believed) unaggressive, unexploitative, and were serenely and uncomplicatedly

occupying their place in the natural order of things. By contrast, the people back home were aggressive, neurotic, obsessed with money, and practiced a religion that justified their violent colonialism and condemned them to lives of sexual unhappiness and industrial and commercial slavery.

The proof of it lay in the Balinese attitude to art. In the West, the artist was considered a rare talented individual set aside from his fellows, nice to have about

the place but slightly odd. The arguments of the English Victorian writer William Morris that all men were artists before industrialism forced the artist onto the edge of things went largely unheeded. But here in Bali was the very situation Morris had described. Everyone painted or carved, danced or played the *gamelan*. Here was paradise indeed!

A DARKER VERSION

There was another, and entirely different, tradition about the real nature of these islands. It didn't refer specifically to Bali, but the archipelago as a whole was seen by some not so much as a paradise but as positively malign. Along the banks of the rivers the trees rotted into the water in a seasonless torpor. Disease was everywhere. The

The unaltering round of life – OPPOSITE: fishing for shellfish near Singaraja; ABOVE: women bearing offerings, on the beach near Goa Lawah.

climate was enervating and oppressive, and here the white man's virtue seemed to wither and die, leaving him a callous and exploitative brute. As for the locals, they might smile, but they were both superstitious and treacherous, and when stung, quick to violence. It's a vision of the islands presented in Szekely's *Tropic Fever* and hinted at in the despairing last chapter of Brian May's *Indonesian Tragedy* (see BIBLIOGRAPHY). But Bali invariably received a better press.

THE HIPPIE TRAIL

In more modern times, the tradition of Bali as a paradise was revived in the sixties for exactly the same reasons that it had been created in the thirties. The criticism of conventional Western society offered by the hippies was identical to that of their more select band of predecessors, and when they voted with their feet to condemn the industrial and commercial societies of the West, many of them ended up on Kuta Beach admiring the sunset, usually with the aid of the local psychedelic mushrooms. It was a mass movement, and their analysis may not always have been well framed, but in its essential points it coincided with that of their predecessors entirely.

THE FUTURE

If the prewar generation only began to establish a rudimentary beach culture, and the sixties travelers were the first to place Kuta on the international tourist map, today surf, sun, sand and sea undoubtedly occupy first place among Bali's tourist attractions. How does this bode for the future of an island whose unique art and religious life, whether or not it's quite what its first modern admirers took it to be, un-questionably places it among the great cultural treasure houses of the world?

To date, Bali's culture has survived quite remarkably, and it may well be that this is not because it has been treated with discretion by tactful, highly educated visitors, but the reverse. Paradoxically, it may have survived because by so many people it has simply been ignored.

And when they have met, the spiritual has often found little difficulty cohabiting with the hedonistic. The surfer who rides the great waves at Ulu Watu 12 hours a day, drunk on Foster's and salt spume, is in a sense as singleminded and loyal to his gods as the girl who carries her offerings on her head at sunset to the village temple, each being in their own way pure.

MOMENTS OF VISION

Sometimes the meeting of the two cultures is more than fortuitous. After I was snatched from the rip current by the Surf Rescue on Kuta Beach, the head of the rescue team asked me if I'd like to attend the anniversary festival of his village temple which happened to be taking place that same evening. Of course I accepted. I knew the Balinese offered up gifts of fruit, cakes and flowers on such occasions, so I asked him what I should bring.

He stood there on the warm sand of the great bay looking out to sea, the long line of volcanoes rising smoothly in the distance. Then he turned to me and smiled.

"The gods have need of nothing," he said quietly.

At the house of Filipino artist Antonio Blanco, Ubud. There is hardly a corner of Balinese life where some indication of hope, some sign of joy can't be found.

Travelers'
Tips

PASSPORTS, VISAS, ETC.

Passports must be valid for six months from date of entry into Indonesia.

You do not need to acquire a visa in advance if you are a passport holder of one of the following countries: Australia (unless you're a journalist), Austria, Belgium, Brunei, Canada, Denmark, Finland, France, Greece, Hong Kong, Iceland, Ireland, Italy, Japan, Luxembourg, Malaysia, the Netherlands, New Zealand, Norway, the Philippines, Singapore, South Korea, Spain, Sweden, Switzerland, Taiwan, Thailand, the United Kingdom, the United States, West Germany and Yugoslavia.

For all the above, passports will be stamped allowing a stay of two months on arrival in Indonesia. You must, however, be in possession of a ticket out of the country (though "purchase of a ticket is also accepted"), and entry must be through one of the following:

Airports: Ambon (Pattimura), Batam (Batubesar), Biak (Fran Kaisiepo), Bali (Ngurah Rai), Jakarta (Halim/Soekarno-Hatta), Kupang (El Tari), Manado (Sam Ratulangi), Medan (Polonia), Padang (Tabing), Pekan-Baru (Simpangtiga), Pontianak (Soepadio).

Sea Ports: Bali (Benoa/Padangbai), Jakarta (Tanjung Priok), Batam (Batu Ampar), Manado (Bitung), Medan (Belawan), Ambon (Yos Soedarso), Semarang (Tanjung Mas), Surabaya (Tanjung Perak).

These visaless two-month stays cannot be extended other than by leaving Indonesia and then re-entering again. This is a common practice, however, and you can fly from Bali to Singapore and back again on the same day with a minimum of fuss.

Nationals of all other countries must obtain their visas in advance; these are of various kinds and can mostly be extended at least once.

Holders of Portuguese passports are, at the time of writing, not allowed to enter Indonesia even if they have somehow or other managed to acquire a visa.

If you do need to renew a visa in Bali, the Denpasar Immigration Office is at Jalan Diponegoro 222, © 2439. It's open from 7 am to 1 pm Monday to Thursday, closes at 11 am Fridays, 12 noon Saturdays, and is shut on Sundays.

CUSTOMS ALLOWANCES

If you are entering Indonesia under the two month visaless arrangement, or for a conference, you may bring with you 150 cigars or 600 cigarettes or 300 grams of tobacco. If you hold a one-week visa you can bring a third of this amount, and a two-week visa, two thirds. All visitors may bring in two liters of alcoholic beverages in opened bottles, a "reasonable quantity" of perfume, and gifts up to a value of US$100. Birds, dogs, cats and monkeys are not allowed into certain parts of Indonesia of which Bali is one.

Customs officials can be difficult in Bali. Some may demand that you leave items such as videos or personal computers at the airport to be collected on departure. Strong protests, however, will usually result in the serial numbers being written in your passport instead.

DRUGS

Don't be tempted to import or use drugs in Bali. Under the Indonesian Narcotic Drugs Law of 1976, it is an offense for anyone to have knowledge of drug use and not pass it on to the police. As for actual possession, amounts are irrelevant, and it is in no way the case that having a small amount constitutes only a minor offense.

Maximum penalties are as follows: for possessing cannabis or cocaine, six years' imprisonment, with a fine of Rp10 million; for possessing "other narcotic drugs," ten years and Rp15 million.

Selling or importing drugs is punishable by a 21-year sentence, or life, with the death penalty available for the second category of substances (though to date this has not been imposed in a drugs case anywhere in Indonesia).

The prison for southern Bali is at Kerobokan, just north of Kuta, and recently there were over thirty foreigners serving sentences there for drugs offenses.

There was a time when Bali was considered a paradise for psychedelic experiences. It is emphatically not so now. Visitors should neither import nor use any narcotic substances there – you may never know who told on you as informers are protected by Indonesian law from identification in court.

Be warned.

HEALTH

There are no obligatory vaccinations required for entry into Indonesia, other than for yellow fever if you have been in an infected area during the previous six days. It's a good idea, though, to consult your doctor and perhaps have an anti-tetanus vaccination anyway before leaving home.

Malaria exists all over Indonesia and, though the risk in southern Bali is small, you should nevertheless play safe and take prophylactic tablets to cover your stay on the island. The most convenient ones have to be taken once a week, beginning before you arrive and continuing for several weeks after you leave. Get advice on the most appropriate brand as resistance to chloroquine has been reported from parts of Indonesia.

Because of the risk of hepatitis, beware of food sold from roadside stalls or carts, and drink only bottled water and soft drinks, or water that has been properly boiled.

Your main enemy is probably the sun. Get into the habit of wearing a hat, avoid sunbathing in the middle of the day, and only lie on the beach for short periods during your first few days. Suntan oils with a high protection factor will help, though it is possible to take these to extremes and negate the whole point of being on a beach in the first place. Just take care, find your own tolerance levels, and don't try to look like a hardened surfer, or a Balinese, after your first afternoon.

If you do get ill, there are local health clinics known as *puskesmas*, but tourists are not expected to use them and you could find yourself being charged distinctly non-local rates for very elementary treatment. It's a better idea to go to one of the Western doctors attached to the Hyatt, Bali Beach or Nusa Dua hotels – they'll almost always see you, even though you're not a guest.

In case of serious illness or injury, it is best to leave Bali as soon as possible for treatment in Singapore or Australia. Local hospitals and clinics are not well equipped.

Mosquito bites do tend to become septic, almost as a matter of course. It's wise to carry some antibiotic ointment for use on these and other more serious cuts and abrasions.

And anyone with professional medical knowledge in Asia will want to carry with him a private medical kit for first aid or for the cases of often horrific skin disease he will inevitably encounter.

CURRENCY

You can bring unlimited amounts of foreign currency into Indonesia but only up to Rp50,000 in Indonesian money, and this latter must be declared on entry.

But there's very little reason for acquiring rupiahs before you arrive in Bali. The exchange kiosk at the airport stays open until after the last flight of the day has arrived, and rates are virtually identical to those offered by the banks and the money changers in Kuta, Sanur, etc. In addition, exchange rates for the rupiah are often not particularly advantageous outside Indonesia.

Rupiahs come in 5, 10, 25, 50 and 100 rupiah coins, and 100, 500, 1,000 and 5,000 notes. The small denomination coins are very rarely seen nowadays. At the time of writing 16 rupiahs bought just US$0.01. There isn't much you can buy for that, even in Indonesia.

Money-changing facilities are found everywhere in the tourist areas of southern Bali, and they offer rates virtually identical to those given by the banks. What the banks are useful for, though, is getting money sent to you in Bali from abroad, and as safekeeping for documents and valuables.

The **Pan Indonesian Bank** (© 51-076-8) on Jalan Legian in Kuta, close to Cheater's Disco, provides both these services. The **Eskpor-Impor Bank** at Jalan Mada 87 in Denpasar will also handle money transactions from abroad for you.

It's a good idea when somebody transfers money to you from abroad for them to send you a copy of the transfer notice to an address other than the bank, just to be on the safe side.

When traveling to villages up-country, make sure you have plenty of small change as large notes can often not be changed away from the tourist areas.

FROM THE AIRPORT

Ngurah Rai is the official name for Denpasar airport, after the hero who led a resistance group against the Dutch in 1946. There's a statue of him at the T-junction at the end of the airport road, where you turn left for Sanur or right for Nusa Dua. The airport is often just referred to as Tuban after the village nearby.

The airport is very close to all the major resorts in southern Bali. In addition, taxi fares are controlled by a system where you pay at a control desk and give the voucher to the driver. The desk is open from before the first till after the last flight of the day. Rates are as follows:

	Non-air-con	Air-con
Kuta	Rp3,200	Rp4,500
Legian	5,000	6,500
Bali Oberoi	7,500	10,000
Denpasar	6,800	9,000
Sanur	8,700	12,000
Nusa Dua	9,200	12,000
Per hour	6,000	8,000

Maximum load is four to a taxi. Insurance is included but extra payment is required for additional destinations.

If you're going to Kuta and really want to economize, you could catch a bemo (daylight hours only). Leave the international terminal through the car park, pass the domestic terminal on your right and continue on till a road leads in from the left. It's about 400 m (1312 ft). Stand at the junction and the bemos (blue transit vans) coming out of the side road will find you. The fare to Kuta is Rp200.

If you've any problems on arriving, try the Airport Information Desk. The attendants are particularly helpful. Ask for Mr Ketut Open: there isn't much about Bali he doesn't know.

ACCOMMODATION

There is every possible type of accommodation available in Bali, but the choice drops dramatically once you leave the southeast.

All the international-standard hotels are in Nusa Dua, Sanur or Kuta. There is *no* accommodation other than five-star hotels in Nusa Dua; a reasonable range, but nothing very cheap, in Sanur; and everything from the most expensive hotel on the island to rooms for US$2 a night in Kuta.

Like everything else in Indonesia, accommodation is excellent value when you're bringing in major foreign currencies. A five-star hotel room in Bali costs approximately half what it would do in a West European or American city.

And, at the other end of the scale, a cheap room in a *losmen* or homestay will almost invariably be clean, have an over-head fan, and look out onto a central garden. It will have a cold-water shower, and breakfast (of tea or coffee with toast and fruit) will be included in the overnight price.

Once you leave this tourist belt, however, you are unlikely to have much

choice as to where to spend the night. There are *losmen* almost everywhere, and even where there are none people will be only too eager to adjust the family arrangements in order to provide you with a room for the night and themselves with some additional income.

There are, of course, subsidiary tourist enclaves, such as at Lovina in the north and Candi Dasa in the east, where there are better-quality small hotels, and there are delightful surprises in the most unexpected places. In Denpasar there are two goodish hotels, and a huge number that are far from prepossessing. And at Ubud there is again a wide range to choose from.

The rates in the body of the text are based on the price of an average double room. Equivalents are:

Inexpensive: under Rp9,000 (US$5.50)
Moderate: Rp9,000-40,000 (US$5.50-24)
Average and above: Rp40,000-90,000 (US$24-55)
Expensive: over Rp90,000 (US$55)

RESTAURANTS

In the Kuta-Sanur area, Indonesian food approaches being a rarity. It's sometimes easier to get a Mexican, Italian or German meal than a Balinese one. You certainly never need eat non-Western food if you don't want to. In Nusa Dua, all the hotels have several restaurants offering food that could well have been prepared in New York, Paris or Rome.

Elsewhere on the island you'll have to put up with what you find. In all the places tourists frequent, attempts will be made to offer Western-style food, but these will often not amount to anything very different from the local fare. But, as with hotels, there are eating-places here and there that are both unexpected and a delight to discover.

Rates in the text are based on the price of a meal for two with one alcoholic drink apiece. But note that alcohol prices are generally at Western levels or above, and a couple more drinks can quickly double the price of any meal.

Inexpensive: under Rp10,000 (US$6)
Moderate: Rp10,000-20,000 (US$6-12)
Average and above: Rp20,000-40,000 (US$12-24)
Expensive: over Rp40,000 (US$24)

It is important to remember that prices at the budget end of the scale are very low. It is possible to eat a simple meal for

The charm of Bali is the charm of the people. There are better beaches on other islands, and less trying climates in other continents. Yet Bali has what perhaps nowhere else has in quite the same way – a wealth of dignified ease.

around Rp1,000 (US$0.60), and to find a *losmen* room for Rp2,000 (US$1.20), almost anywhere in Bali outside the southern tourist belt. Add fifty percent for these popular areas.

AIRLINE OFFICES

Most flights into and out of Denpasar are by Garuda Indonesia, even though many of them are operated jointly with other airlines. You book with, say, Singapore Airlines but find you are on a Garuda plane at least for the last leg.

Garuda International's head office in Bali is at Jalan Melati 61. ✆ 27825 and 22028. They also maintain offices in the following hotels:
Bali Beach Hotel, ✆ 8241/8511 ext 130.
Kuta Beach Hotel, ✆ 5179.
Nusa Dua Beach Hotel, ✆ 971444/ 971210 ext 729/730.
Garuda's Lost and Found Office is on 51171 and 51011 ext 278/238.

Other international airline offices are in the following locations:
Cathay Pacific, Bali Beach Hotel. ✆ 8576.
KLM, Bali Beach Hotel. ✆ 8511 ext 588.
Malaysian Airlines System, Bali Beach Hotel. ✆ 8511 ext 165.
Qantas Airways, Bali Beach Hotel. ✆ 8331; airport office: 51472.
Singapore Airlines, Bali Beach Hotel. ✆ 8511 ext 587.
Scandinavian Airlines System, Bali Beach Hotel. ✆ 8141/8063.
Thai International, Bali Beach Hotel. ✆ 8141/8063.

Two Indonesian airlines operating domestic flights are:
Bouraq, Jalan Sudirman 19a. ✆ 24656; airport office: 51011 ext 255.
Merpati Nusantara, Jalan Melati 57. ✆ 22864; reservations, 25841; airport office: 51374/51011 ext 253.

TRAVEL AGENTS AND TOURS

The following travel agents are based in Bali and can arrange tours of the island. Tours are usually one-day round trips, taking in three or four celebrated sites and including lunch.
Bali Lestari Indah, PO Box 312, Jalan Raya Sanur 130, Denpasar. ✆ 24-000/26099. Telex: 35252 BATUR DPR.
Balindo Star, PO Box 455, Jalan W. R. Supratman 114X, Denpasar 80237. ✆ 25372/22497/28669. Telex: 55261 STAR DPR.
Celong Indonesia, PO Box 43 DPS –Denpasar, Jalan Raya Sanur. ✆ 28227/28325. Telex: 35128 CELONG DPS.
Natrabu, Jalan Kecubung, Denpasar. ✆ 25448/25449/23452/24925. Telex: 35144 NATRABU DPS.
Pacto, PO Box 52 DPS – Denpasar, Jalan Tanjung Sari, Sanur. ✆ 8247/8248/8249. Telex: 35110 PACTO BALI.

Tours of longer than a day are unusual, but anything can be arranged on Bali. Express an interest to one of the drivers used by your hotel, or any of the talented freelancers waiting about at Kuta's Bemo Corner, and you will have a personalized package tour with a very special price assembled for you within the quarter hour.

OVERLAND TO JAVA

Numerous bus companies operate on the Denpasar-Surabaya route, often overnight. A good one is **Artha Mas**, with offices at Jalan Diponegoro 23 in Denpasar (✆ 25042) and the Hotel Bali, Jalan Makam Peneleh 77 in Surabaya (✆ 471984). The fare includes the short ferry crossing from Gilimanuk to Banyuwangi, and a free meal at one of the stops. Videos are screened on the bus during the first part of the journey.

There is no railway on Bali, but from Banyuwangi on the tip of Java a fast and modern service runs to Jakarta. The best Indonesian trains are luxurious and a pleasure to travel on, and the through express to Jakarta is one of these. Local trains are a different matter, however, though extraordinarily cheap. Information about connections to Surabaya and Yojyakarta, as well as the special train to Jakarta, can be obtained at the railway's office at Jalan Diponegoro 172 in Denpasar.

TRANSPORT

CAR RENTAL

Renting a car is one way of seeing Bali, and the Suzuki Jimny, handy for the rougher roads, is particularly popular. These and other vehicles can be rented from the following:

Avis Car Rental, Jalan Raya Kuta. ✆ 51474.

Bali Beringin Rent Car, Jalan Raya Airport 2. ✆ 51356.

Bali Car Rental, Jalan Bypass Ngurah Rai. ✆ 8359/8550.

Bali Central Rent-a-car, Kuta Beach. ✆ 51313/51195.

Bali Happy, Jalan Raya Tuban. ✆ 51-954.

Bali Purnama, Jalan Melasti, Legian. ✆ 51901/51792.

C.V. Karya Int., Utara Bali Hyatt. ✆ 8334/8521.

Europ Car, Trio Bali Int., Jalan Raya Sanur/Pandu 5. ✆ 25830/26830.

You must, of course, be in possession of an up-to-date international driver's license to drive on the island.

BEMO CULTURE

Bemos are a way of life, and one of the easiest ways of seeing something of the life of the ordinary Balinese people. It's a common occurrence to ride in these small, open-backed vans in the company of sacks of rice, chickens and even a couple of pigs.

Fares are fixed, and everyone except the tourist knows them. It isn't a bargaining situation. Nevertheless, as it seems eminently reasonable to take from a foreigner money he seems to want to throw away, larger amounts than necessary are usually accepted if you don't keep your wits about you. The best plan, if you don't know the correct fare, is to watch what the locals hand over, and to keep a stock of small coins so that you can offer the exact

fare, or what you judge might well be the right fare, without leaving it up to the conductor to decide whether or not to give you any change. There are no tickets.

Nor are there timetables. The bemo drivers hire their vehicles on a day-to-day basis and consequently have to do their best to recoup the hire charge and make what profit they can. Bemos leave when they're full, rarely before. They can't be relied on running after dark, except on the Denpasar-Kuta run; in some places, such as the mountain villages of Penelokan and Kintamani, or in the country around Ubud, the last bemos of the day tend to leave well before five. Check on your outward journey so as not to take any chances.

You can sit in the front alongside the driver if you like; there's no extra charge

Renting a motorbike is easy in Bali – but you do need a licence.

(ie. it isn't "first class"). You pay the conductor (or *kernet*) as you leave for the distance you've traveled. There are no fixed stops, other than at each end of the route; when you want to get out, shout "Stopa!" or just "Stop!" To get on, wave one down – you won't have any trouble as they're on permanent lookout for custom, with the *kernet* calling out the bemo's destination to pedestrians as it passes. If you aren't sure if the bemo you hail is going where you want to go, just ask. No one will mind if you stopped them for nothing – they're as hungry for travelers as bees for nectar. And crowd in wherever you can: no bemo was ever too full to take another passenger.

You won't have been using bemos long before some driver suggests you charter one. This means you decide where it goes and use it like a taxi. He's an independent operator and is under no obligation to ply any particular route. It's a good way to get to somewhere off the beaten track fast, but it won't be especially cheap, and the driver will hope you're not going to mind if he picks up extra passengers in the normal way as well. But the system has all the charm and convenience of earlier times in more "developed" countries when travel, like buying and selling, was a simple matter of an arrangement between those who needed and those willing to fulfill the need. The existence of the need made certain that someone would move in to satisfy it. Bemos are undoubtedly bumpy and hot, but riding in one often conveys something unavailable in air-conditioned coaches – the romance of travel.

MOTORBIKES

An estimated ten thousand visitors a year rent motorbikes while on Bali. It's an excellent way to see the island, and especially good for getting away from the main tourist trail. Take extra care on the main roads, however, where the traffic in recent years has become very heavy.

Most people rent from **Bakor Motor**, an agency that is in effect a collective of motorbike owners. Register with them, tell them the kind of machine you require, and one plus its owner will quickly appear at your address, ready to negotiate a deal. The deal is then registered by Bakor, and you take out an insurance policy, also through the agency, for something around Rp30,000 a month. Any subsequent dispute with the owner can be settled through Bakor.

If you don't have an international driver's license, validated for motorcycle use, you will have to get a special permit to ride a motorbike in Bali. You go to the Denpasar Police Office (Bakor will take you) and undergo a test involving recognizing road signs and showing you can drive your bike around a figure-of-eight without putting a foot down on the ground.

Bakor's main office is in Kuta, with branches in Ubud and Sanur.

MEDIA

TELEVISION AND RADIO

There is only one TV station in Indonesia at present. There's an hour of English programs every night, from 6 to 7, with the news at 6:30 pm.

And twiddle the knobs of your hotel-room radio and you should find a program in English beginning at 9 pm nightly.

NEWSPAPERS

There are three English-language papers published in Jakarta, *The Indonesia Times*, *The Jakarta Post* and *The Indonesia Observer*. They are normally on sale in southern Bali from about mid-morning on the day of issue.

The Indonesia Times advertises a price "in Jakarta" of Rp300, but expect to pay twice this in Bali. This increase represents air-freight costs plus the extra palms the paper's passed through. Remember, too, the boy who will probably sell you the paper depends on the difference between what you give him and what he must give his employer for his only income. Don't begrudge him the odd Rp100 – it's only US$0.06, after all.

There's also an English-language news magazine published weekly. It's called *Indonesia*.

COMMUNICATIONS

TELEPHONE

The telephone is not one of Bali's great strengths. Subscribers tell stories of "secret sharers" who occupy their line from time to time and push up the bill even when they are temporarily disconnected for non-payment. The visitor is more likely to come across unobtainable numbers and times when hotel staff are unable to get a line at all. It can often take as many as 20-30 tries to get through to busy exchanges.

There are no coin boxes that work; the best tactic is to use a phone in one of the bigger hotels.

Tones are as follows: ready for dialing – a continuous tone; ringing – long repeated tones; occupied – short repeated pips.

Area codes are frequently advertised, but in reality you will almost certainly have to go through the operator, and invariably so for calls abroad. You may, though, manage to get through direct *from* outside *to* numbers in the Denpasar area (which includes Kuta, Sanur and Nusa Dua). The area code here is 0361.

The following may be useful:
Operator 100
Fire 113
Police 110
Ambulance 118, 26305
International operator 102
Time 103

International inquiries 106
Directory inquiries 108
Complaints 117

This last is the number you are most likely to need.

Time

Bali, in common with Java, is seven hours ahead of GMT, and three hours behind Australian Eastern Standard Time. It is 13 hours ahead of New York and 16 hours ahead of California.

MAIL

To find the Post Office, ask for *Kantor Pos*. In Kuta, it's close to the Night Market, with a very efficient sub-office in Jalan Bakungsari close to the junction with the main Denpasar-Tuban road. In Sanur, it's a little way inland, on Jalan Segara. Denpasar Post Office is inconveniently placed on the road to Sanur, away from the town center.

Many people have their mail sent care of American Express. Their office is in the Bali Beach Hotel at Sanur.

As in many Asian countries, it is advisable to try to see the clerk actually cancel your stamps. Relative money values are such that the postage on a heavy letter overseas can equal a day's pay for an Indonesian worker; consequently the temptation to remove your stamps might very occasionally be irresistible. The present writer has never heard of this happening in Bali, however.

Register any important or valuable mail.

Many "postal agents" will sell stamps, accept your mail and post it for you and they are generally quite reliable.

Express is extremely cheap and should save a couple of days. At the time of writing, postal rates were as follows:

Airmail postcard
Australia and Asia Rp375
Europe Rp475
America and Africa Rp600

Letters up to 10g
Australia and Asia Rp450
Europe Rp550
America and Africa Rp700

Aerograms
Australia and Asia Rp400
Europe Rp525
America and Africa Rp650

Parcels up to 1 kg
Australia and Asia Rp19,300
Europe Rp39,300
America and Africa Rp39,300

There is a telex office on Jalan Legian, Kuta, very close to the side street leading to Peanuts discotheque.

CLOTHING

The government issues a poster detailing undesirable and preferred modes of dress. What it is saying, behind the now out-moded depiction of undesirable forms of Western dress, is that tourists should remember that this is someone else's country and their conventions should be adhered to. The beach and adjacent streets are one thing, but the rest of the island is very much another.

It's particularly important to wear reasonably formal dress when visiting government offices. This may differ from what's considered formal back home, and you should simply look at what the better-off Indonesians wear to get an idea of their expectations of you. Short sleeves, for instance, are perfectly acceptable for men, and ties are rare. But long trousers, shoes as op-posed to sandals or thongs, and above all a neat, newly pressed general appearance are essential ingredients of the style.

For women, modesty is the keynote. Remember that it's going to be hot, and sometimes very hot, and that loose-fitting clothes are much cooler than close-fitting ones. Cotton is also cooler than artificial fabrics.

To enter a Balinese temple, one must wear a sarong and a sash. Most will rent these for a fee, but it is simpler to buy them for a few thousand rupiah and carry them with you.

A moment's thought is worth pages of advice. You would never dream of turning up to a funeral at home in beachwear, but it's astonishing how many tourists turn up in shorts and a T-shirt to a Balinese crema-tion.

BARGAINING

Be prepared to bargain for most things in Bali. It's the most natural, and surely the most ancient, system in the world. If you want to buy, and he wants to sell, why should anything as rigid as a fixed price come between you?

You can even bargain for your hotel room, along the lines of "What price will you give me if I stay a week?" or "What's the discount, seeing as it is low season?" It may turn out to be inappropriate, but it's necessary to understand the Balinese will never be surprised – to them, it's fixed prices that are unnatural, the foreign impor-tation.

The secret of successful bargaining is to get your offer in first. Once the ven-dor has named a price, it would involve too much loss of face to accept any-thing much less than sixty percent of it. Nevertheless, for you to make the first offer, and then go on to describe it im-mediately as your last price, is to go against the whole spirit of the business, and is guaranteed to remove the smile off any In-donesian face. You've simply broken the rules, and been very rude into the bargain because you've left him no room to maneuver.

There are places, though, where you don't bargain – restaurants and the larger shops for instance. And the Balinese don't bargain over bemo fares, though you might find yourself having to if you haven't managed to find out the correct fare in advance. But wherever you're dealing with someone who's master of his own business, whether it's a girl hawking T-shirts on the beach or a boy offering to drive you around on the back of his motorbike, bargaining is the accepted, and expected, way to go about things.

Also, remember this is a culture where sellers frequently approach you with their wares. This often annoys visitors, on Kuta Beach for example, but remember that *any* answer, even "No thanks," is often taken as an indication of at least some degree of interest. A silent shake of the head – and a smile – will normally see you aren't disturbed any longer.

TIPPING

Tipping isn't really the custom on Bali, but this shouldn't prevent you rewarding someone who has provided you with a useful service. You might, for example, tip your room boy after an extended stay but not after a short one. There's no need at all to tip in restaurants.

WATER SPORTS

SURFING

Surfing is a world all of its own. It's a religious cult with its own hermetic language and sacred locations.

Bali is considered one of the world's ideal surfing venues because of the consistency of its waves, breaking in exactly the same way for hours on end, and because when conditions make the ocean on one beach flat, there are other beaches only a short drive away where the surfing is likely to be stupendous.

The classic place for surfing is Ulu Watu. Here the waves are of world class and surfing films and international competitions have been held here. Close by is Padang Padang. Neither venue is for the

beginner, but both are well off the usual tourist routes and ideal for watching the masters of the art at play.

At Kuta the waves are smaller (though they can still be too dangerous to surf at all). Here, the classic locations are halfway between Kuta and Legian – "Half-Legian" – Kuta Reef, and Canggu and Medowi further north up the beach.

In addition, some surfers make the trip out to Nusa Lembongan, and, in the rainy season, surf off the reef at Sanur.

SAILING AND WINDSURFING

Sailing and windsurfing are available on the sheltered eastern side of the islands during the dry season. Inquire at any of the larger hotels at Nusa Dua or Sanur. For more reasonable rates than these are likely to offer you, ask along Sanur Beach, or at the Rai or Mentari Restaurants at Benoa. Sailing is on local outriggers or the occasional Hobie Cat catamaran.

Fishing *prahu* on the beach at Sanur. They will even take you across the Badung Strait to Jungutbatu on Nusa Lembongan – a trip that seems frightningly far for such simple craft.

DIVING

There's superb diving on the remote island of Menjangan in the northwest. The Lovina beaches in North Bali have good snorkeling, and both snorkeling and diving are available on Nusa Lembongan.

SAFETY IN SURF

Lives are lost every year on Bali's beaches. See the KUTA section (p.130) for details of the work of the Surf Rescue teams.

Remember – never go more than waist-deep unless you are a very strong swimmer. If a current is pulling you out to sea, don't try to swim against it, but sidewards out of it. And if in distress of any kind, raise a hand above your head – it's the international signal for help and represents your best chance of being rescued.

RELIGION

There are several churches and mosques in Denpasar, and in addition various large hotels hold services. Details are as follows:

Catholic
Churches
Jalan Kepundung, Denpasar
St. Francis Xavier, Kuta/Tuban
Services in hotels
Bali Beach Hotel, Legong Room, Saturday 5 pm
Bali Hyatt, Hibiscus Room, Saturday 6 pm
Bali Sol, Conference Hall I, Sunday 5 pm
Nusa Dua Beach Hotel, Garuda Room, Sunday 6 pm

Protestant
Churches
Protestant Maranatha, Jalan Surapati, Denpasar
Seventh Day Adventist, Jalan Surapati, Denpasar

Pentecostal, Jalan Karna, Denpasar
Services in hotels
Bali Beach Hotel, Sunday 6 pm

Islamic
Mosques
Raya Mosque, Jalan Hasanudin, Denpasar
Annur Mosque, Jalan Diponegoro, Denpasar
Taqwa Mosque, Jalan Supratman, Denpasar
Services in hotels
Al-Hissan Mosque, Bali Beach Hotel

ETIQUETTE

The Balinese are very polite and visitors should try to be the same. A few simple points will see you a long way toward fitting in with their environment.

- Give and take everything with the right hand. The left is considered unclean.
- Never touch anyone on the head, even a child.
- Don't photograph people bathing in rivers, and in other circumstances ask first, if only with a smile and a gesture.
- Don't beckon someone toward you with your index finger as it's considered very rude.
- Wear a sash around your waist whenever you go into a temple, and at a ceremony such as a cremation don't wear shorts, thongs and a skimpy T-shirt. No one will be the slightest bit amused if you wear a sarong; they will be delighted, and many people will compliment you on your taste.
- Pointing at people, and standing with your arms folded or with your hands on your hips are widely considered vulgar.

The Balinese, incidentally, never say "thank you" in the normal run of things on receipt of a gift. If they do so, it will be because they have been trained to do it by the hotel where they work. Similarly, it's impolite to call someone simply by his first name in Bali, but hotel workers have been trained to accept this slight along with other imported barbarisms.

SEX

Inevitably, male visitors will be offered prostitutes in Bali, especially in Kuta, but it is to the eternal credit of the Balinese that they will very rarely be from Bali itself. Touts will whisper "Balinese girl, very young" to you on a dark night, but they will almost certainly be from one of the other islands and the touts are confident no foreigner will ever know the difference.

LANGUAGE

The language generally known as Bahasa Indonesia ("the Indonesian language") is actually Malay. The language of Bali is Balinese, a difficult tongue with different forms for addressing the various social classes. All Balinese now learn Bahasa Indonesia in school, and as it is very easy, and can be used throughout Indonesia as well as in Malaysia, it's the one you should try to master at least a few phrases of. There are no articles, no plurals, and no tenses, and the verb "to be" isn't used (*Bali bagus* = Bali *is* beautiful).

Pronunciation is easy and straightforward: the important point is that Indonesian is easy to *hear*. Most people can pick up the sounds and general intonation parrot-like almost at once. In this, Indonesian contrasts strongly with most other Asian languages which, with their complex systems of tones, are very difficult.

Because it's so easy, it's immense fun to try. It's also very poetic. Start off with some of the following:

Good Morning. *Selamat pagi.* ("May your action be blessed this morning.")

How are you? *Apa khabar?* ("What's the news?")

I'm fine. *Khabar baik.* ("The news is good.")

Thank you. *Terima kasih.*

It's a pleasure. *Kembali.*

Goodbye (when *you're* leaving). *Permisi.* (The reply to this is *Mari.*)

What is your name? *Siapa namamu?*

My name is ... *Nama saya...*

Please speak slowly. *Tolong bicara pelan-pelan.*

I'll come back later. *Saya akan kembali nanti.*

May I come in? *Boleh saya masuk?*

This is good! *Ini bagus!*

Is it safe to swim here? *Anam berenang disini?*

How much is this? *Berapa haga ini?*

About... *Kira kira...*

1, 2, 3, 4, 5... *Satu, dua, tiga, empat, lima...*

...6, 7, 8, 9, 10. *...enam, tujuh, delapan, sembilan, sepuluh.*

11, 12, 13... *sebelas, dua belas, tiga belas* (*belas* = ten)

20, 30... *dua puluh, tiga puluh* (*puluh* = tens)

100 *seratus*

200, 300... *dua ratus, tiga ratus* (*ratus* = hundreds)

1,000 *seribu*

2,000, 3,000... *dua ribu, tiga ribu* (*ribu* = thousands)

1,000,000 *seratus ribu*

And in answer to the eternal question "Where are you going?" try "*Makan ingin*" ("To eat the wind").

A helpful little booklet is John Barker's *Practical Indonesian*, available all over Bali.

CONSULATES AND EMBASSIES

Seven countries maintain consulates, consular agencies, representatives or honorary consuls in Bali. These are:

Australia Jalan Raya 146, Sanur. ℂ 25997/25998. Jalan Legian, Kuta. ℂ 51997.

Italy Jalan Bypass Ngurah Rai, Padang Galak, Sanur. © 8372/25858.
Japan Jalan Raya 124, Sanur. © 25611.
Sweden Jalan Segara, Sanur. © 8231/-8407.
Switzerland Swiss Restaurant, Jalan Legian, Kuta. © 8535/51735.
United States Jalan Segara, Sanur. © 8478.
West Germany Swiss Restaurant, Jalan Legian, Kuta. © 8535/51735.

The following are the phone numbers of the various embassies in Jakarta:

Afghanistan ©33169/342677
Algeria © 49310/352694
Argentina © 45368/338088
Australia © 23109/331856
Austria © 45811/248568
Bangladesh © 21690/324850
Belgium © 48719/351682
Bolivia © 21362
Brazil © 58378
Brunei © 583051 ext 1613
Bulgaria © 43926/346725
Burma © 20440/327204
Canada 584031
Chile © 584309/587611
Columbia © 517717/516446
Czechoslovakia © 40538/344994
Denmark © 48615
East Germany © 28908
Egypt © 45325/345572
Finland © 516980
France © 32807/332403
Hungary © 587521/587522
India © 581850/588182
Iran © 31391
Iraq © 55016/355017
Italy © 47907/348339
Japan © 24308
Kampuchea © 467836
Malaysia © 32864/336647
Mexico © 33909/337974
New Zealand © 30620/330680
North Korea © 46457
Norway © 54556/354557
Pakistan © 50576/350577
Panama © 41995

Papua New Guinea © 584604
Philippines © 46786
Poland © 20509
Portugal © 54521/365111
Rumania © 49524
Saudi Arabia © 46342
Singapore © 48761
South Korea © 58081/512309
Spain © 25996
Sweden © 32306/333061
Switzerland © 517468
Syria © 44334/354570
Thailand © 43762/348221
Turkey © 36809
United Kingdom © 30904/331039
United States © 60360
Union of Soviet Socialist Republics © 21477
Vatican © 41142
Vietnam © 47325
West Germany 882414/882491
Yemen © 45225
Yugoslavia © 33720

SELECTED INDONESIAN MISSIONS ABROAD

Australia
Canberra, © 73-3222
Darwin, © 819352
Melbourne, © 6907811
Perth, © 219821
Sydney, © 264-2976/2195/2323
Austria
Vienna, © 342533/4/5
Belgium
Brussels, © 771-2013/4
Canada
Ontario, © 236-7403/5
Toronto, © 5916613/5916461
Vancouver, © 682-8855/8
Denmark
Copenhagen, © 624422/ 625439
France
Paris, © 2881999
Marseilles, © 713435
Greece
Athens, © 8814082
Hong Kong   © (5) 7904421/8

India
Delhi, ✆ 602352/602343/ 602308
Italy
Rome, ✆ 475-9251/2/3
Japan
Tokyo, ✆ 441-4201-9
Kobe, ✆ 321-1654
Sapporo, ✆ 251-6602
Malaysia
Kuala Lumpur, ✆ 421011/421141/ 421-228/ 421354/421460
New Zealand
Wellington, ✆ 758695/9
Netherlands
The Hague, ✆ 469796
Singapore ✆ 7377422
South Korea
Seoul, ✆ 782-5116/8
Spain
Madrid, ✆ 4130294/4130594
Switzerland
Bern, ✆ 440983/5
Thailand
Bangkok, ✆ 2523125/2523177

United Kingdom
London, ✆ 499-7661
USA
Washington DC, ✆ 293-1745
Chicago, ✆ 938-0101
Honolulu, ✆ 524-4300
Houston, ✆ 626-3291
Los Angeles, ✆ 383-5126/8
New York, ✆ 879-0600
San Francisco, ✆ 474-9571
West Germany
Bonn, ✆ 310091
Dusseldorf, ✆ 353081
Frankfurt, ✆ 231740
Hannover, ✆ 1032150
Munich, ✆ 294609

The enjoyment is evident as these girls proceed to a purification ceremonyon Kuta Beach.

Bibliography

BAUM, Vicki *A Tale from Bali* (1937). Reissued in paperback by OUP. Translated from German, a novel set between 1904 and 1906 when the Dutch were extending their control over the island.

COVARRUBIAS, Miguel *The Island of Bali* (1937). Reissued in paperback by OUP. The classic account. Essentially a systematic survey of Balinese life and culture interspersed with personal recollections from this Mexican painter who made two extended visits to the island.

DALTON, Bill *Indonesia Handbook* (2nd edn 1980). Moon Publications, Chico, Ca. Though ostensibly for the back-packing budget traveler, this voluminous and outspoken account has, almost despite itself, reached classic status. Inevitably lacking detail on Bali, it is the guidebook to take with you to the rest of Indonesia.

EISEMAN, Fred B. *Bali, Sekala and Niskala* (2 vols, 1985, 1986). The leading authority on everything Balinese, Eiseman is a retired American academic chemist who spends six months of every year on Bali. These two books, contain a vast range of information on everything from Balinese scripts (which Eiseman is computerizing) to the manufacture of concrete telephone poles on the Bukit. Breathtaking.

EISEMAN, Margaret and Fred *Flowers of Bali* (1987). An identification aid to some of the commoner flowers of the island, with color photographs.

KERTONEGORO, Madi *The Spirit Journey to Bali Aga, Tenganan Pegringsingan* (1986). Harkat Foundation, Bali. A whimsical, eccentric but amusing account of some legends from the Candi Dasa/Tenganan area.

KOCH, C.J. *The Year of Living Dangerously* (1978). Reissued by Grafton paperbacks. An imaginative and sympathetic novel set in Jakarta at the time of the fall of Sukarno in 1965. An enormously interesting insight into Indonesian life and politics.

LEURAS, Leonard, and LLOYD, Ian R. *Bali, the Ultimate Island* (1987). Times Editions. The ultimate Bali picture-book, with additional photographs by Cartier-Bresson and other old masters.

MABBETT, Hugh *In Praise of Kuta* (1987). January Books, Wellington. Breaking with the "cultural treasurehouse" tradition, this is a collection of short essays on Bali's much-maligned tourist capital.

MATHEWS, Anna *The Night of Purnama* (1965). Reissued in paperback by OUP. A low-key account of living in the village of Iseh, north of Klungkung, culminating in the eruption of nearby Agung in 1963.

MAY, Brian *The Indonesian Tragedy* (1978) RKP, London and Boston. An in-depth, but also personal, look at modern Indonesian politics from a journalist who worked for many years in the country. Disenchanted but passionate. A surprisingly good read.

McPHEE, Colin *A House in Bali* (1947). Reissued by OUP in Oxford in Asia paperback series. McPhee was an American composer who went to Bali to study the *gamelan* (which he describes as "a shining rain of silver"). The first Westerner to build a house at Kuta, his book is sensitive and intelligent.

POWELL, Hickman *The Last Paradise* (1930). Reissued in paperback by OUP. One of the very early books. Rather specifically American, it is by turns sardonic and lushly poetic. Describes the *gamelan* as "the muffled laughter of forgotten gods." Richly readable.

RAMSEYER, Urs *The Art and Culture of Bali* (1977). Fribourg. Translated from German, a quasi-academic survey. Rather like a vast museum catalogue with innumerable black-and-white photographs. Dispensable.

TANTRI, K'tut *Revolt in Paradise*. Reissued in Indonesia, in English, Indonesian and Dutch, by Gramedia Paperbacks. A high-spirited account of the adventures of a young American woman who went to Bali alone in the 1930s, helped set up Kuta's first hotel, was imprisoned by the Japanese, and became famous throughout the region as "Surabaya Sue", freedom-fighter with the Indonesians. Born Vannine Walker, her original pseudonym was Muriel Pearson.

Limited to only five books, I'd take Koch, Powell, May, Covarrubias, and McPhee, and get hold of Eiseman and Tantri when I got to Bali.

Quick Reference A – Z Guide to Places and Topics of Interest with Listed Accommodation, Restaurants and Useful Telephone Numbers

A accommodation, general 103, 200
  prices of 201
Agung, see Mt Agung 164
Air Panas 153–154
Air Panas, accommodation
  Balai Seni Topabungkah 154
airlines serving Bali 202
  Bouraq, (✆ 24656) 202
  Cathay Pacific, (✆ 8576) 202
  Garuda International, (✆ 27825 and
    22028) 202
  KLM, (✆ 8511 ext 588) 202
  Malaysian Airlines System,
    (✆ 8511) 202
  Merpati Nusantara, (✆ 22864) 202
  Qantas Airways, (✆ 8331) 202
  Scandinavian Airlines System,
    (✆ 8141/8063) 202
  Singapore Airlines, (✆ 8511 ext 587) 202
  Thai International, (✆ 8141/8063) 202
airport
  facilities and transportation to and
  from 200
Amlapura 169, 175
  Puri Amsterdam 175
  The Palace 175
  water palaces 176–178
Amlapura, accommodation
  Homestay Balakiran 175
Amlapura, restaurants
  Restaurant Tirta-Ayu 176
Anturan 106
art, Balinese 82
artists, Western, in Bali 19
arts and crafts 81–89
  mask making 86
  masks 86
  silverware 89
  stone carving 86
  weaving 89
  wood carving, places to see and buy 85
  wood carvings 85
B Bali, diminutive kingdoms of 17
Balinese culture
  origins of 15–17
Balinese names 31
Balinese opera 67
Bangli 150
  access 151
  Pura Kehen (temple) 151
Bangli, restaurants
  Artha Sastra 151
Banjar
  access 108

Buddhist Temple 108
  hot springs 108
  hot springs at 107
banks
  Pan Indonesian Bank (✆ 51076-8) 200
  Ekspor-Impor Bank 200
Banyuwedang
  hot springs 188
Batur 154–156, 158–159
  Temple of Ulan Danu 160
Batur Lake 152
Batur Village 152
Batur, restaurants
  Puri Selera 158
Bedugul 103, 165–166
  Botanical Gardens 166
  Lake Braton 166
  Ulu Danu temple 166
Bedugul, accommodation
  Bali Handara Country Club 166
  Bedugul Hotel and Restaurant 166
bemo culture 203
Benoa 119
Besakih 158, 160–164, 166
  Mother Temple 161
bird orchestras 80–81
Bona
  dance dramas at 67
Buddhism 17
C calendar, Balinese use of a variety of 43
Candi Dasa 171–175
  Bug Bug 172
Candi Dasa, accommodation
  Amarta Homestay 174–175
  Candidasa Beach Bungalows and
    Restaurant (✆ Amlapura 180) 173
  Natia Homestay 174–175
  Pondok Bambu Seaside Cottages
    (✆ Amlapura 169) 173
  Puri Bali 173
  Puri Pandan (✆ Amlapura 169) 173
Candikuning
  Ulu Danu Temple 166
car rentals 203
  Avis Car Rental, (✆ 51474) 203
  Bali Beringin Rent Car, (✆ 51356) 203
  Bali Car Rental, (✆ 8359/8550) 203
  Bali Central Rent-a-car, (✆ 51313/
    51195) 203
  Bali Happy, (✆ 51954) 203
  Bali Purnama, (✆ 51901/51792) 203
  C.V. Karya Int.,(✆ 8334/8521) 203
  Europ Car, (✆ 25830/26830) 203
caste system in Bali 29, 31–32, 34–35,

41, 49, 53
Celuk, silverware center 89
Central Bali 146–150
cigarettes, local 98
Cikik
  Directorate General of Forest Protection
    and Nature Conservation (PPHA) 187
climate 12–13
clothing, advice on dress 206
cockfighting 80
Consulates and Embassies 209
  Australia, (℃ 51997) 209
  Italy, (℃ 8372/25858) 210
Consulates in Sanur
  Japan, (℃ 25611) 210
  Sweden, (℃ 8231/8407) 210
  Switzerland, (℃ 8535/51735) 210
  United States, (℃ 8478) 210
  West Germany, (℃ 8535/51735) 210
cremation 32, 35, 40, 48, 50, 53, 71, 77
  ceremony 48–53
cricket fighting 80
currency 199
customs allowances 198

D dance, Balinese 64, 67
   dances, main Balinese 67
     Arja 67
     Baris Gede 67
     Baris Pendet 68
     Barong 68
     Barong Landong 71
     Calon Arang 71
     Gambuh 71
     Janger 71
     Jauk 71
     Joged 71
     Kebiyar Duduk 72
     Kecak 72
     Kupu Kupu Carum 72
     Legong 72
     Mendet 74
     Oleg Tambulilingan 74
     Panyembrama 74
     Prembon 74
     Ramayana Ballet 74
     Rejang 74
     Sanghyang Dedari 74
     Sanghyang Jaran 74
     Topeng Pajegan 74
     Topeng Panca 74
     Wayeng Wong 74
   Denpasar 112–115
     Academy of Dance, Indonesia 115
     Annual Bali Arts Festival 115
     Badung Government Tourist Office
       (℃ 23399 and 23602) 115
     Bali Government Tourist Office
       (℃ 22387   and 26313) 115
     bemo stations 116
     Conservatory of Performing Arts 115
     Immigration Office (℃ 2439) 115
     Museum Bali 114
     National Art Center 114
     Pura Jagatnatha 114
     shopping 115

Tanah Lapang Puputan Badung 114
Denpasar, accommodation
  Bali Hotel (℃ 5681/5) 115
  Pamecutan Palace, (℃ 23491) 115
  Wismasari Inn (℃ 22437) 115
Denpasar, restaurants
  Puri Selera Restaurant 115
Dewi Sri, rice goddess 28, 43
dieties, Balinese 43
diving, general advice 208
drama, Balinese 61, 64, 71–72, 74, 77
drugs 198
Dutch, the, in Bali 18
  arrival 18

E East Bali 166–178
   Embassies and Consulates, Indonesian mis-
     sions abroad 210–211
     Athens, (℃ 8814082) 210
     Bangkok, (℃ 252-3125/252-3177) 211
     Bern, (℃ 440983/5) 211
     Bonn, (℃ 310091) 211
     Brussels, (℃ 771-2013/4) 210
     Canberra, (℃ 73-3222) 210
     Chicago, (℃ 938-0101) 211
     Copenhagen, (℃ 624422/ 625439) 210
     Darwin, (℃ 819352) 210
     Delhi, (℃ 602352/602343/ 602308)
       210
     Dusseldorf, (℃ 353081) 211
     Frankfurt, (℃ 231740) 211
     Hannover, (℃ 103-2150) 211
     Hong Kong (℃ (5) 7904421/8) 210
     Honolulu, (℃ 524-4300) 211
     Houston, (℃ 626-3291) 211
     Kobe, (℃ 321-1654) 210
     Kuala Lumpur, (℃ 421011/421141/
       421-228/ 421354/421460) 211
     London, (℃ 499-7661) 211
     Los Angeles, (℃ 383-5126/8) 211
     Madrid, (℃ 413-0294/413-0594) 211
     Marseilles, (℃ 713435) 210
     Melbourne, (℃ 690-7811) 210
     Munich, (℃ 294609) 211
     New York, (℃ 879-0600) 211
     Ontario, (℃ 236-7403/5) 210
     Paris, (℃ 288-1999) 210
     Rome, (℃ 475-9251/2/3) 210
     San Francisco, (℃ 474-9571) 211
     Sapporo, (℃ 251-6602) 210
     Seoul, (℃ 782-5116/8) 211
     Singapore ℃ 737-7422)0) 211
     Sydney, (℃ 264-2976/2195/2323) 210
     The Hague, (℃ 469796) 211
     Tokyo, (℃ 441-4201-9) 210
     Toronto, (℃ 5916613/591-6461) 210
     Vancouver, (℃ 682-8855/8) 210
     Vienna, (℃ 342533/4/5) 210
     Washington DC, (℃ 293-1745) 211
     Wellington, (℃ 758-695/9) 211
   Embassies, Jakarta
     Afghanistan, (℃33169/342677) 210
     Algeria (℃ 49310/352694) 210
     Argentina (℃ 45368/338088) 210
     Australia (℃ 23109/331856) 210
     Austria (℃ 45811/248568) 210

Bangladesh (✆ 21690/324850) 210
Belgium (✆ 48719/351682) 210
Bolivia (✆ 21362) 210
Brazil (✆ 58378) 210
Brunei (✆ 583051 ext 1613) 210
Bulgaria (✆ 43926/346725 210
Burma (✆ 20440/327204) 210
Canada 584031) 210
Chile (✆ 584309/587611) 210
Columbia (✆ 517717/516446) 210
Czechoslovakia (✆ 40538/344994) 210
Denmark (✆ 48615) 210
East Germany (✆ 28908) 210
Egypt (✆ 45325/345572) 210
Finland (✆ 516980) 210
France (✆ 32807/332403) 210
Hungary (✆ 587521/587522) 210
India (✆ 581850/588182) 210
Iran (✆ 31391) 210
Iraq (✆ 55016/355017) 210
Italy (✆ 47907/348339) 210
Japan (✆ 24308) 210
Kampuchea (✆ 467836) 210
Malaysia (✆ 32864/336647) 210
Mexico (✆ 33909/337974) 210
New Zealand (✆ 30620/330680) 210
North Korea (✆ 46457) 210
Norway (✆ 54556/354557) 210
Pakistan (✆ 50576/350577) 210
Panama (✆ 41995) 210
Papua New Guinea (✆ 584604) 210
Philippines (✆ 46786) 210
Poland (✆ 20509) 210
Portugal (✆ 54521/365111) 210
Rumania (✆ 49524) 210
Saudi Arabia (✆ 46342) 210
Singapore (✆ 48761) 210
South Korea (✆ 58081/512309) 210
Spain (✆ 25996) 210
Sweden (✆ 32306/333061) 210
Switzerland (✆ 517468) 210
Syria (✆ 44334/354570) 210
Thailand (✆ 43762/348221) 210
Turkey (✆ 36809) 210
Union of Soviet Socialist Republics
    (✆ 21477) 210
United Kingdom (✆ 30904/331039) 210
United States (✆ 60360) 210
Vatican (✆ 41142) 210
Vietnam (✆ 47325) 210
West Germany (✆ 882414/882491) 210
Yemen (✆ 45225) 210
Yugoslavia (✆ 33720) 210
emergency and useful telephone
    numbers 205
Operator (✆ 100)
Fire (✆ 113)
Police (✆ 110)
Ambulance (✆ 118, 26305)
International operator (✆ 102)
Time (✆ 103)
International inquiries (✆ 106)
Directory inquiries (✆ 108)
Complaints (✆ 117)
etiquette 208

Europe, trade with 18
F festivals
    locations and dates 47
    Nyepi 27
    temple, dates of 47
    tourist information on 74
festivals, major
    Nyepi 47
flora and fauna 13
foods
    Balinese festive 90–92
    basic Balinese dishes 90
    betel chewing 98
    cold drinks 93
    festive dishes 90
    local specialities 93
    prices in restaurants 201
    the coconut 97
    tropical fruits, the main attractions 94
G gambong (orchestra) 48–50, 53
gamelan (orchestra) 61–62, 64, 67, 77
Gelgel 168–169
    Royal Temple 169
Gilimanuk
    ferry terminal for Java 187
Goa Lawah
    Bat Cave and temple 169
    primitive salt factory 170
H health 199
herbal medicine
    Jamu 98
Hinduism 14, 29, 32, 39–41, 54, 58, 79
    introduction to Java 14
I Indonesia
    birth of Republic of 20
    political institutions of 20
Iseh 164
Islam 17
    arrival of 17
J Jagaraja 109
Java 14, 17
    bus service, Artha Mas, ✆ 25042 202
    access, overland 202
Javanese civilizations 17
Jimbaran 120
Jimbaran Bay 116, 120
Jimbaran village 116
Jimbaran, accommodation
    Hotel Puri Bali (✆ 25442) 120
Jungutbatu 186
Jungutbatu, accommodation in
    Johnny's Bungalow 186
    Losmen Agung 186
    Wayan Tarci Losmen 186
    Wayan's Nasa Lembongan Bungalows
        (✆ 51875 and 51170) 186
K Kabutambahan 109
Kalibukbuk 106–107
    see restaurants, under Lovina
Kamasan 168–169
Kedisan 157–158
Kintamani 158–160
Kintamani, accommodation
    Puri Astina 160

Kintamani, restaurants
  Kintamani Restaurant   158
Kintomani   109
Klumpu   183
Klungkung   166–167
  floating palace   166
  food stalls   167
  market   167
Klungkung, accommodation
  Ramayana Palace Restaurant and Hotel   167
Kubutambahan
  temple   109
Kusamba   180
  boat departures for Nusa Penida and Nusa
Lembongan   169
Kuta   124–135
  beach   124
  Bemo Corner   128
  history   130
  Legian   126
  Night Market   128
  shopping   135
  Surf Rescue   127, 130
Kuta, accommodation
  Agung Beach Bungalows (✆ 51263/4)   132
  Bali Mandira Cottages (✆ 51381)   132
  Bali Oberoi (✆ 51061)   132
  Ida Beach Inn Bungalows (✆ 51205
  and 51934)   132
  Kartika Plaza (✆ 51067-9)   132
  Fourteen Roses (✆ 51156 and 51835)   132
  Kuta Beach Hotel (✆ 51361)   132
  Kuta Palace Hotel (✆ 51461/2 and
  51879)   132
  Kuta Village Inn (✆ 51059)   132
  Legian Beach Hotel (✆ 51711)   132
  Pertamina Cottages (✆ 51161)   130
  Poppies Cottages (✆ 51059 and
  51149)   132
  Puspa Beach Inn (✆ 51988)   132
  Ramayana Seaside Cottages
  (✆ 51864-6)   132
Kuta, nightlife
  Bruna's   135
  Casablanca   134
  Cheaters ✆ 51638)   134
  Chez Gado Gado   134
  Double Six   135
  Il Pirata   135
  Peanuts   134
  Rivoli   134
  SC Club   134
  Tuak Bar   135
  Yani's   135
Kuta, restaurants
  Bali Indah Seafood restaurant   133
  Batu Karang Beach Bar and Res-
  taurant   134
  Daruma Japanese Restaurant
  (✆ 23906)   134
  Dayu 1 (✆ 51498)   134
  Depot Kuta (✆ 51155)   134
  Double Six   134
  Glory   133
  La Barong   133

  Made's Warung   133
  Paul Nyoman's Bar and Restaurant/
  Pizzeria   134
  Poppies   133
  Swiss Restaurant (✆ 51735)   133
  The Green House (✆ 51193)   134
  TJ's   133
  Wayan's Tavern (✆ 51578)   134

L Labuanhaji Falls   108
Labuhanlalang
  ferry point for Menjangan Island   187
Lake Braton   166
language   209
  Balinese   23
  national   23
  useful phrases   209
Lembongan village   186
Lombok, access   170
Lontar   172
Lovina   106
  access   106
Lovina, (Kalibukbuk) restaurants
  Hungarian Restaurant   106
  Nirwana Restaurant   106
Lovina, accommodation
  Aditya (✆21781)   106
  Ayodya   106
  Banualit Beach Inn (✆ 41889)   106
  Baruna Beach Inn (✆ 41252)   106
  Janur Dive Inn   106
  John's Dive Inn   106
  Nirwana   106
  Parma Beach Homestay   106
  Suki Jati Reef (✆ 21952)   106
  Astina   106

M magic and witchcraft   54, 71
marriage customs   34–35, 54
Mas
  famous wood carving shop at   85
  wood carving center   85
masks, Balinese   48, 74, 86
  making of   86
media   204
Menanga   160
Mengwi   138–139
  Water Temple   138
Mengwi, restaurants
  Water Garden Restaurant (✆ 4318 and
  6863)   139–140
Menjangan Island   187
  scuba diving   187
monkeys, wild, in Bali   13
motorbike rentals
  Bakor Motor Kuta, Ubud and Sanur   204
Mt Abang   152
  climbing   158
Mt Agung   152, 162, 164
  climbing   162
  Door of   164
  guides   162
Mt Batur   138, 151–152
musical instruments, Balinese   61

N Negara
  water buffalo races at   189
  water buffalo races, information,

(© 23399 and 23602   189
North Bali   103–109
    access   103
Nusa Dua   116–123
Nusa Dua, accommodation
    Bali Club Med (© 971520-5)   118
    Hotel Bualu (© 71310)   118
    Nusa Dua Beach Hotel (© 71210)   118
    Putri Bali (© 71020 and 71420)   118
Nusa Lembongan   180, 186
    access   180
Nusa Lembongan, accommodation
    Johnny's Bungalow   186
    Losmen Agung   186
    Wayan Tarci Losmen   186
    Wayan's Nasa Lembongan Bungalows
        (© 51875 and 51170)   186
Nusa Penida   116, 180, 186
    access by boat from Kusamba   169
    cliff stairways   186
    Goa Karangsari cave   182
    guides to   183
    limestone plateau   182
Nusa Penida, access   180
Nyuling, Moslim village of   175

P   Padangbai   166, 169–171
    Biastugel Beach   171
    boat services to other destinations   171
    ferry terminal for Lombok   170
    speedboat service to Nusa Penida   180
Padangbai, accommodation
    Padangbai Beach Inn   170
    Rai Beach Inn   170
Padangbai, restaurants
    Johnny's   170
    Kendedes Restaurant   170
passport and visa requirements for Indonesia
    198
Peed   183
    temple at   183
Pejeng   149
    Archaeological Museum   149
    Crazy Buffalo Temple   149
    Pura Panataram Sasih temple   149
Penelokan   151–152, 155, 157–158, 160
    Batur Lake   152
    Mt Batur   151
Penelokan, accommodation
    Lake View Homestay   151
Penulisan   160
    temple   160
post offices and postal service   205
public transport   203
Pujang
    painted carvings center   85
Pujung   147
    banana-tree carvings   147
Pulaki
    Monkey Temple   107
Pulau Serangan (Turtle Island)   119–120
    water sports   119
Pulau Serangan (Turtle Island), restaurants
    Mentari Bar and Restaurant   119
    Rai Seafood Restaurant   119
Pulau Serangan, restaurants in   119

puppets
    performances of   77
    types of   78
R   Rambutsiwi
    temple at   188
religious services   208
Rendang   164
restaurants
    see also food, prices
    see under place name
rice
    cult of   28
    Dewi Sri, goddess of   28, 43
S   sailing and windsurfing
    general advice   207
Sampalan   182
Sampalan, accommodation
    Bungalows Pemda   182
Sangeh   140
    Monkey Forest   140
Sangsit
    Pura Beji Temple   108
Sanur   110–111, 180, 186
    Batu Jumbar   112
    Museum Le Mayeur   112
    shopping   112
Sanur, accommodation
    Alit's Beach Bungalows (© 8567 and
        8560)   110
    Bali Beach Hotel (© 8511   111
    Hotel Tandjung Sari (© 8441)   111
    Mars Hotel (© 8236°   111
    Natour Sindhu Beach Hotel
        (© 8351/2)   111
    Queen Bali Hotel (© 8054)   111
    Sanur Beach Hotel (© 8011)   111
    Santrian Beach Cottages (© 8009)   111
    Segara Village Hotel (© 8407/8 and
        8231)   111
    Taman Agung Inn (© 8549)   111
Sanur, nightlife   112
    Bali Hyatt disco   112
    Number One disco   112
    Subec disco   112
Sanur, restaurants
    Italian Terrazzo Martini (© 8371)   111
    Karya Bar and Restaurant (© 8376)   111
    Kesunasar (© 8371)   111
    Kita Japanese Restaurant (© 8158)   111
    Ronny's Pub and Restaurant (© 8370)   111
    Yuyu Restaurant (© 8009)   111
Sawan   109
    access   109
    gong making   109
Sayan   146
Sayan, accommodation
    Sayan Terrace Cottages   146
scuba diving   118, 187
Sebatu   147
    public baths   147
Sebudi   164
    access   164
Sebuluh   183
    cliff stairway near   183
Sembiran   109

temple   110
sex   209
shopping, general advice   206
Sidemen   164
Singaraja   103–105
    Tourist Information Bureau   104
Singaraja, accommodation in
    Ramiyana Hotel (© 41108)   106
slave trade   19
Songan   154
    temple at   154
South Bali   136–145
spice trade   18
spirits, belief in   14
Sukat   164
surfing
    general advice   207
surfing and surf rescue   208
T Tampaksiring   147
    Gunung Kawi   147
    Sukarno Palace   147
    Tirta Empul   147
Tanah Lot   138
    access   138
    temple at   138
Tanjung Benoa   116, 119
taxis   *see* bemo culture
Tegalalang   147
telephone service   205
temple
    Balinese, typical layout of a   42
Tenganan   171
    craft shop   172
    shopping   172
Tenganan, weaving center   89
The Bukit   116–123
Tirtagangga   176
tourism, begining of   19
Toyapakeh   182
transport, public   104, 116, 134
    from Denpasar   116
travel and tour agents   202
    Bali Lestari Indah, (© 24000/26099)   202
    Balindo Star, (© 25372/22497/28669)   202
    Celong Indonesia, (© 28227/28325)   202
    Pacto, (© 8247/8248/8249   202
trees, species of in Bali   13
tropical fruits, range of   94–96
Trunyan   152, 157
    access by boat   157

Trunyan, accommodation
    Segara Homestay and Restaurant   157
U Ubud   103, 140
    access   141
    Antonio Blanco's House   144
    dog orchestra   144
    Elephant Cave   150
    Legong Dance   140
    Museum Neka   143
    Palace, dance dramas at   64
    puppet theatre   141
    Puri Lukisan Museum   143
Ubud, accommodation
    Ardjuna's Inn (© 22809)   142
    Hans Snel's Siti Bungalows
        (© 28690)   142
    Hotel Tjampuhan (© 28871)   141
    Jati Homestay   142
    Munut Bungalows   142
    Puri Saraswati   142
    Rama Sita Pension   142
    Sudharsana's Bungalows   142
    Tjanderi's   142
Ubud, restaurants
    Jati Restaurant   143
    Lotus Cafe   142
    Menara Restaurant   143
    Murni's Warung   143
    Nomad Wine Bar and Restaurant   143
    Puri's Snackbar   143
    Raya Coffee House   143
Ujung   176
    access   176
Ulu Watu   116, 120
    Pura Luhur Ulu Watu   122
    surfing   122–123
V volcanoes   11, 13, 151
    Agung   11
    Batur   11
W water sports
    general advice   207
West Bali   187–189
    National Park   187
    National Park, entry permits for   187
Y Yeh Pulu   149
    frieze   149
Yeh Sanih   109
Yeh Sanih, accommodation
    Bungalow Puri Sanih   109